D0809614

SPECTRUM

Word Study and Phonics

Grade 6

Published by
Frank Schaffer Publications®

Frank Schaffer Publications®

Spectrum is an imprint of Frank Schaffer Publications.

Send all inquiries to:
Frank Schaffer Publications
8720 Orion Place
Columbus, Ohio 43240-2111

Spectrum Word Study and Phonics—grade 6

ISBN 0-7696-8296-0

2 3 4 5 6 POH 11 10 09 08 07

NAME ____________________

Lesson 1.1 Hard and Soft **c** and **g**

The letters **c** and **g** can make a hard sound, as in *candle* and *ground*. When followed by **e**, **i**, or **y**, they can make a soft sound, as in *gerbil* and *fancy*.

Read each bold word. Decide whether it has a hard or soft sound and underline the word beside it that has the same sound.

1. **gateway**	gypsy	began	fragile
2. **coliseum**	receipt	cider	because
3. **tragic**	forgotten	legend	gopher
4. **gardenia**	gesture	segment	vegetable
5. **collaborate**	electric	sincerely	cinder

On the line next to each bold word below, write **HC** (hard **c**), **HG** (hard **g**), **SC** (soft **c**), or **SG** (soft **g**) to show which sound the word contains.

1. A **comet** ____________ is a body in the solar system that is made of **ice** ____________, dust, and gases.
2. The word *comet* has its **origins** ____________ in Latin and **Greek** ____________. It means *hairy one* or *hairy star*.
3. Before **scientists** ____________ had determined what comets were, many people **considered** ____________ them to be bad omens.
4. A comet that travels close to the sun is visible from Earth as an **object** ____________ that **glows** ____________ with a long, streaming tail.
5. The **forces** ____________ of the sun, including pressure and solar wind, **cause** ____________ a comet's tail to form from **gas** ____________ and dust.
6. For this reason, the tail **generally** ____________ points away from the sun.
7. Halley's comet, which appears approximately **once** ____________ every 76 years, was last seen in 1986.

Table of Contents, continued

Table of Contents Grade 6

NAME ______________________

Lesson 1.1 Hard and Soft **c** and **g**

Read the paragraphs below. Write the words that contain the hard and soft **c** and **g** sounds in the correct columns. You do not need to list the same word more than once unless it can be listed in more than one category.

Anyone who has ever seen a geyser is sure to agree that geysers are one of the wonders of the natural world. A geyser is a type of hot spring that shoots streams of water and steam directly into the air. Geysers exist in only a few regions on Earth, including Japan, Iceland, and New Zealand. The largest geyser field in the world, however, is located here in the United States at Yellowstone National Park. Approximately 400 geysers steam, bubble, and gurgle at Yellowstone!

Geysers occur when water seeps underground and is heated by magma, or molten rock. The steam and boiling water are trapped by cooler water in tube-like passages underground. Pressure continues to build, and eventually water and steam shoot out of the geyser in a giant burst. The remaining water in the geyser cools down so that it is no longer boiling, and the eruption ends. As the water seeps back into the earth, the whole cycle begins again.

The eruptions of some geysers are predictable. Yellowstone's Old Faithful erupts about every 80 minutes and shoots as much as 8,500 gallons of boiling water nearly 200 feet in the air. It's quite a spectacle to see, and tourists are often on hand to witness the amazing event—at a safe distance.

Hard **g**: ______________ ______________ ______________

______________ ______________ ______________

______________ ______________ ______________

Soft **g**: ______________ ______________ ______________

____

Hard **c**: ______________ ______________ ______________

______________ ______________ ______________

______________ ______________ ______________

______________ ______________ ______________

Soft **c**: ______________ ______________ ______________

NAME ____________________

Lesson 1.2 The Sounds of s

The letter **s** can make several different sounds.
- It can make the /s/ sound, as in *salute*.
- It can make the /z/ sound, as in *positive*.
- It can make the /sh/ sound, as in *insurance*.
- It can make the /zh/ sound, as in *usually*.

Read each set of words below. On the line, write the letters of the two words in which **s** makes the same sound.

1. ______	**a.** fusion	**b.** sandbox	**c.** museum	**d.** casual
2. ______	**a.** reasoning	**b.** sanctuary	**c.** includes	**d.** tissue
3. ______	**a.** scurry	**b.** composed	**c.** intermission	**d.** surely
4. ______	**a.** cheese	**b.** trustworthy	**c.** tremendous	**d.** measure
5. ______	**a.** vision	**b.** explanations	**c.** scuba	**d.** Asia
6. ______	**a.** superior	**b.** headquarters	**c.** sugary	**d.** pleasing
7. ______	**a.** observation	**b.** pleasurable	**c.** treasure	**d.** tension
8. ______	**a.** harness	**b.** erosion	**c.** sophomore	**d.** ours

Read the words in the box. Write each word under the correct heading below.

expansion basketball refusal sugar preservative frustrate
composition postpone precision tissue division
visionary permission newspaper casually restless

/s/ sound	/z/ sound	/zh/ sound	/sh/ sound
______	______	______	______
______	______	______	______
______	______	______	______
______	______	______	______

NAME ____________________

Lesson 1.2 The Sounds of s

On the line, write the **s** sound you hear in each bold word. Choose from /s/ (as in *soup*), /z/ (as in *these*), /zh/ (as in *invasion*), and /sh/ (as in *mission*).

Pam Muñoz Ryan has written many different types of books. Writing about a **diverse** ____________ group of **topics** ____________ keeps things fresh and interesting for her. She gets her ideas from moments in **history** ____________, stories she hears on the **news** ____________, and sometimes even from her family. For example, Ryan's picture book *Amelia and Eleanor Go for a Ride* is **based** ____________ on a flight that Amelia Earhart and Eleanor **Roosevelt** ____________ took over Washington D.C. In the novel *Esperanza* ***Rising*** ____________, Ryan tells a fictionalized **version** ____________ of her **grandmother's** ____________ journey from Mexico to the United States.

Ryan also keeps an idea file. She jots down notes on **scraps** ____________ of paper, **napkins** ____________, and the backs of receipts. When she is ready to begin a new project, she can flip through her file and look for story ideas that are **unusual** ____________ or ones that she feels especially **passionate** ____________ about.

When Ryan speaks to children at **libraries** ____________ or schools, she tries to give them a **realistic** ____________ picture of what it's like to be a writer. She doesn't want them to get the **impression** ____________ that a writer's life is strictly **glamorous** ____________. She **reminds** ____________ her audience that working from home isn't **usually** ____________ the **leisurely** ____________ pastime that some imagine it to be.

NAME ____________________

Review Hard and Soft **c** and **g** and the Sounds of **s**

Complete each riddle below with a word from the box. The word you choose should make sense in the riddle and contain the correct sound shown in parentheses.

centipede	refrigerator	Antarctica	Cinderella	frogs	because

Q: Why is a river rich?

A: ________________ it has two banks (hard **c**)

Q: Why did the boy close the ________________ door quickly? (soft **g**)

A: Because he saw the salad dressing

Q: Where do frozen ants come from?

A: ________________ (hard **c**)

Q: What do you get if you cross a ________________ and a parrot? (soft **c**)

A: A walkie-talkie

Q: What year do ________________ like best? (hard **g**)

A: Leap year

Q: Why was ________________ thrown off the baseball team? (soft **c**)

A: Because she ran away from the ball

Read the word pairs below. Underline the **c** or **g** sound you hear in both words.

1.	gingerbread	geometric	hard **g**	soft **g**
2.	juggling	guardian	hard **g**	soft **g**
3.	village	generally	hard **g**	soft **g**
4.	climate	counterclockwise	hard **c**	soft **c**
5.	circulation	reception	hard **c**	soft **c**
6.	convey	occasional	hard **c**	soft **c**

NAME ____________________

Review Hard and Soft **c** and **g** and the Sounds of **s**

Unscramble the bold letters and write the word that matches each clue. The hint in parentheses will tell you which sound of **s** the word contains.

1. unique; not common **uusalun** (/zh/) ____________
2. garments; covering for the body **oceslth** (/z/) ____________
3. protection against loss from fire or death **isurncena** (/sh/) ____________
4. an antonym for *negative* **tipsiove** (/z/) ____________
5. a small spoon **onastepo** (/s/) ____________

Circle the 4 words below that contain the /sh/ sound of **s** and underline the 14 words that contain the /z/ sound of **s**. Do not mark the same word twice.

Dear Diary,

My grandparents gave me a season pass to the art museum for a birthday present this year. It's only four subway stops away from our new apartment, so I can visit as frequently as I like. I've been there several times on field trips, but it is so large, that I think it would take a whole lifetime to know every piece of art. The new expansion will be complete this spring, and I can't wait to see what has changed.

When Isabel and I go this weekend, I'd like to spend some time looking at the work of the Impressionists. In Mr. Yang's class, we recently learned about the issue that a group of artists had in France during the late 1800s. The French Academy was powerful, and they pressured artists to create certain types of work. The group that would later become known as the Impressionists had their own vision of what art could be. Maybe someday I'll have the pleasure of seeing my own artwork hanging proudly on those same walls.

NAME ____________________

Lesson 1.3 Consonant Digraphs

A **digraph** is a blend of two consonants that form a new sound.
- The digraph **sh** makes the /sh/ sound in *egg**sh**ell.*
- The digraph **ch** can make the /ch/, /sh/, or /k/ sound, as in ***ch**arcoal, **ch**auffeur,* and ***ch**emistry.*

Read the sentences below. On each line, write the sound (/sh/, /ch/, or /k/) the digraph makes in the bold word.

1. In **March** ____________, Alena's cousin **Chris** ____________ came to visit.
2. Alena's family had just adopted **Charlotte** ____________, a bloodhound.
3. "She's a bit **shy** ____________," Alena advised her cousin as she **unlatched** ____________ the **leash** ____________.
4. **"She's** ____________ beautiful," commented Chris. "Did you **research** ____________ dog breeds before you **chose** ____________ her?"
5. Alena nodded. "The **chef** ____________ at my stepdad's restaurant told us about a **shelter** ____________ in **Chicago** ____________ that rescues bloodhounds."
6. "The skin around the eyes and ears captures scents. Bloodhounds have a **sharp** ____________ sense of smell and are excellent tracking dogs."
7. "What kind of **character** ____________ do they have?" asked Chris.
8. "They tend to be **cheerful** ____________ and easygoing," replied Alena.
9. "She doesn't like **chipmunks** ____________ or men with **mustaches** ____________," continued Alena with a grin, "but other than that, she's been in a **chronic** ____________ good mood since we got her."

NAME ____________________

Lesson 1.3 Consonant Digraphs

- The digraph **th** can make the unvoiced sound (/th/), as in ***th**umb*, and the voiced sound (/<u>th</u>/), as in *bo**th**er*.
- The digraph **wh** can make the /hw/ sound, as in ***wh**itewash*, and the /h/ sound, as in ***wh**olesale*.
- The digraph **ph** makes the /f/ sound, as in ***ph**otocopy*.

Read the clues below. On the line, write the word from the box that matches the clue and has the sound listed in parentheses. Then, find each word in the word search puzzle. Words may be written forward, backward, or diagonally.

theater	Philippines	northern	whimper	sympathy	wholesome	pharmacy

1. a place where people go to watch a movie (/th/) ____________________
2. an antonym for *southern* (/<u>th</u>/) ____________________
3. a country in southeast Asia that has thousands of islands (/f/) ____________________
4. healthful; nutritious (/h/) ____________________
5. a feeling of pity or sorrow for another person (/th/) ____________________
6. a weak, whining sort of cry (/hw/) ____________________
7. a place where people go to buy prescription medicine (/f/) ____________________

y	e	h	a	n	o	r	t	h	e	r	n	v	e
t	p	h	i	l	i	p	p	i	n	e	s	n	m
o	h	n	t	c	a	s	x	w	b	t	n	n	o
g	a	y	r	e	b	e	w	h	u	a	p	m	s
f	r	r	y	o	a	x	e	i	w	e	n	b	e
y	m	f	g	d	l	l	o	m	b	h	z	j	l
h	a	f	e	w	s	y	m	p	a	t	h	y	o
o	c	l	h	y	r	e	q	e	v	c	d	s	h
k	y	t	u	n	c	w	e	r	b	q	a	k	w

NAME ____________________

Lesson 1.3 Consonant Digraphs

The digraphs **ck**, **ng**, and **gh** can come in the middle or at the end of a word.
- The digraph **ck** makes the /k/ sound, as in *spe**ck**led*.
- The digraph **ng** makes the /ng/ sound, as in *amazi**ng***.
- The digraph **gh** can make the /f/ sound, as in *cou**gh**ed*.

Complete each sentence below with a word from the box. Circle the digraphs **ck**, **ng**, and **gh** in the words you use.

scoring	block	rough	entering	surprising	hockey	puck
playing	enough	increasing	opposing	wearing	stick	

1. ____________ is a team sport played on ice by players ____________ skates.

2. It is not really ____________ that hockey is most popular in regions of the world that stay relatively cold, such as Canada, Finland, and Russia.

3. Because a rubber disc called a ____________ can fly at speeds of more than 100 miles per hour, hockey can be a ____________ and dangerous game.

4. Even plenty of protective equipment isn't always ____________ to keep a player safe.

5. A goaltender's job is to keep the puck from ____________ the net and thus keep the ____________ team from ____________ a point.

6. The goalie may ____________ a shot with his or her body, which is well padded with protective gear, or he or she may use a hockey ____________ as the rest of the players do.

7. Most ice hockey teams are comprised of men, but women have played the game since at least the 1800s. Today, the number of women ____________ the sport is rapidly ____________.

NAME ______________________________

Lesson 1.3 Consonant Digraphs

Read the paragraphs below. On each line, write the digraph (**sh**, **ch**, **th**, or **ng**) that correctly completes the bold word.

Few people would argue that life in America today isn't fast-paced, noisy, and sometimes ______**aotic**. Things are different, ______**ough**, for a group of Americans called the **Ami**______. If you live in a Midwestern state, like Ohio, Indiana, or Kansas, you might be familiar with the Amish. They came to America in the early 1700s **seeki**______ religious freedom, and their way of life has remained relatively **un**______**anged** since then.

The more traditional Amish are members of the Old Order. They ______**un**, or reject, many conveniences of modern-day life. For example, many Old Order Amish ______**oose** not to use electricity in their homes. ______**ey** travel by horse and buggy instead of **usi**______ automobiles. They farm and are able to produce **mu**______ of their food ______**emselves**.

The Amish are known for their **stro**______ sense of community. Their barn-**raisi**______**s** are a famous example of what can be **accompli**______**ed** with cooperation. Hundreds of men work **toge**______**er** to raise a barn for one family. For the Old Order Amish, this means working **wi**______**out** power tools. The women have a similar sense of cooperation and community when they **ga**______**er** to make **pat**______**work** quilts at **quilti**______ bees.

The Amish are resistant to ______**ange** and remain separate from mainstream society in many ways. Living simply without outside influences is important to their way of life. Family, ______**ildren**, work, community, and spirituality are cornerstones of Amish life. Can you see any similarities between your life and the Amish way of life?

NAME ______________________________

Lesson 1.4 Silent Consonants

In some consonant pairs, one letter is silent.
- The letter **k** is silent when it comes before **n**, as in ***kn**eel.*
- The letter **w** is silent when it comes before **r**, as in ***wr**eath.*
- The letter **c** can be silent when it follows **s**, as in ***sc**issors.*
- The letter **b** can be silent when it follows **m**, as in *to**mb**.*

Fill in the blank in each sentence below with a word from the box. Circle the silent letter in the word.

knight	breadcrumbs	knapsack	wrapper	scenic	thumb

1. The secret to Aunt Lulu's meatloaf is using ____________________ made from homemade sourdough bread.
2. The hiker filled her ____________________ with food, water, and a map.
3. Primates are similar to humans in their use of the opposable ____________________.
4. The Hahns decided to take the ____________________ route through the mountains, even though it added a couple of hours to their trip.
5. Although any free man could become a ____________________ during the Middle Ages, it was generally men from wealthy families who received this honor.
6. The plastic ____________________ covering the CD was difficult to remove.

Read each bold word. Circle the word beside it that has the same sound as the underlined letters.

1. **thu<u>mb</u>**	timber	clumsy	thimble
2. **<u>kn</u>ickers**	kayak	kaleidoscope	nightmare
3. **la<u>mb</u>**	comb	member	mumble
4. **<u>wr</u>ath**	wholesale	roundtrip	woodwind
5. **<u>sc</u>ience**	sabotage	collision	insurance

NAME ______________________

Lesson 1.4 Silent Consonants

The interview below contains 18 words that have the silent consonant pairs **kn**, **wr**, **sc**, and **mb**. Circle the words and draw a line through each silent letter.

Vijay Mehta: When did you first know that you wanted to be a singer and songwriter?

Carson Bell: That's an interesting question. I came from a tightly-knit family, and as a child, my brothers and I spent a great deal of time listening to music. We imitated what we heard, and we eventually started creating our own music.

VM: So you always knew you wanted to write music or somehow be involved in the music industry?

CB: No, it was actually a much longer road for me. I was taking the scenic way home from work one night, when I did something dumb. I had a paper cut on my thumb, and I tried to look for a bandage in the glove compartment while I was driving.

VM: What happened?

CB: Well, I wrecked my car, but luckily I didn't do too much damage to myself. When I climbed out of the car, my left wrist hurt pretty badly and I had broken my kneecap, but I was okay.

VM: Did the accident have an impact on your life?

CB: It absolutely did. I enjoyed my job and working in the field of science, but I didn't feel the same passion for it as I had for music. I wrestled with the decision of what I really wanted to do with my life. The scenes from my childhood kept replaying themselves over and over in my mind.

VM: Is that when you went out on a limb and changed your career path?

CB: Yes, and I've never regretted my decision or felt that I had made the wrong choice. I think that knowledge of yourself and the things that are a priority to you are essential to feeling happy and fulfilled.

NAME ____________________

Lesson 1.5 More Silent Consonants

When two or three consonants appear together, one letter is sometimes silent.
- The letter **g** can be silent when it comes before **n**, as in ***g**nome*.
- The letter **d** is silent when it comes before **g**, as in *fu**d**ge*.
- The letter **h** is silent when it follows **r**, as in ***rh**ombus*.
- The letter **t** is silent when it comes before **ch**, as in *ha**tch***.
- The letters **gh** can be silent, as in *si**gh**t*.

Read each clue below. The word that matches the clue is written in bold beside it, but the letters are scrambled. Unscramble the letters, and write the word on the line. Hint: Each word will contain a silent consonant pair.

1. perfume **ogcolne** ____________
2. the sound a person makes when exhaling **hsig** ____________
3. a regular, repeated musical beat **mrythh** ____________
4. to trade or exchange **ciwtsh** ____________
5. an animal that has a single horn on its head **osrinohcer** ____________
6. great pleasure or joy **lidegth** ____________
7. to promise or swear **lpgeed** ____________
8. from another country **eigforn** ____________
9. a type of small ax **thaceth** ____________

Read each word below. Find a rhyming word in the box and write it on the line. Then, cross out the silent letter or letters.

thighs	pitcher	hutch	assign	straight	hedge	rhyme	gnaw

1. cries ____________
2. claw ____________
3. richer ____________
4. incline ____________
5. touch ____________
6. pledge ____________
7. wait ____________
8. climb ____________

NAME ______________________________

Lesson 1.5 More Silent Consonants

Read the sentences below. Complete each bold word with one of these silent letter combinations: **gn**, **dg**, **rh**, **tch**, or **gh**.

1. **He______ehogs** are insectivores, or animals whose diets consist mostly of insects.
2. Before Heath's soccer team began their afternoon practice, the coach led them through a series of warm-up **stre______es**.
3. Sasha helped **desi______** and paint the colorful sets for the class play.
4. Cody helped his dad roll out the **dou______** to make his favorite dessert—strawberry-**______ubarb** pie.
5. In November, Clay had to **resi______** from his position as class president because his family was moving to Missouri.
6. Every summer, Desi and Gabby visit their grandmother in **______ode** Island.
7. Last year, Grandma Nell and the girls worked together to make a **pa______work** quilt for the new baby.
8. When Uncle Ross joined the Peace Corps, he had no idea which **forei______** country he'd be living in for the next two years.

Read each word in bold below and circle the silent letter combination. On the line, write the letter of the word beside it that contains the same combination.

1. ______	**wedged**	**a.** passage	**b.** trudging	**c.** village
2. ______	**rhapsody**	**a.** resemblance	**b.** radioactive	**c.** rhythmic
3. ______	**uptight**	**a.** neigh	**b.** coughed	**c.** thimbles
4. ______	**assignment**	**a.** sagging	**b.** signoff	**c.** assistance
5. ______	**sketching**	**a.** hopscotch	**b.** bleacher	**c.** spinach
6. ______	**judging**	**a.** courage	**b.** college	**c.** knowledgeable
7. ______	**limelight**	**a.** enough	**b.** high	**c.** August
8. ______	**crutches**	**a.** chimpanzee	**b.** cherished	**c.** stitching

NAME ______________________

Lesson 1.6 Ti and Ci

The letters **ti** and **ci** can stand for the /sh/ sound, as in *cau**ti**ous* and *magi**ci**an.*

Read the paragraphs below. Circle the 14 words that contain the /sh/ sound spelled **ti**. Underline the three words that contain the /sh/ sound spelled **ci**. You do not need to mark the same word twice.

The Mayan civilization was at its strongest between A.D. 250 and A.D. 900. It existed in what is today Guatemala, Belize, Mexico, Honduras, and El Salvador. For many years, the Mayan people were somewhat of a mystery to the historians and archaeologists who studied them. *What could have made such a powerful and advanced nation decline so drastically?* they wondered.

The Maya were proficient in agriculture and practiced the cultivation of maize (a type of corn), beans, squash, peppers, avocados, and pineapples. They had an advanced system of irrigation and also used other farming techniques, like rotating crops and building terraces.

There were more than 40 Mayan cities, and at one time, the population may have reached two million. The Maya used a system of hieroglyphic writing, similar to Egyptian hieroglyphics. The Mayan hieroglyphs, as well as inscriptions carved in rock, are important sources of information for modern-day researchers.

The Maya are considered to have been the most advanced ancient civilization in the Western Hemisphere. What caused their decline? It may have been vicious wars, natural disasters, or a disease that wiped out large portions of the population. About 800,000 people today speak Mayan languages. Many modern Maya still live an agricultural lifestyle like their ancestors did. Their preservation of the Mayan culture and traditions in modern society give it the potential to be passed along for generations to come.

NAME ______________________________

Lesson 1.6 Ti and Ci

Read the sentences below. Fill in each blank with the letters **ti** or **ci**.

1. By the day of the **audi______on**, Madeline had bitten off all her fingernails and had moved on to nervously twirling a piece of hair around her finger.
2. Her favorite teacher, **Patri______a** Mooney, had made the **sugges______on** that Madeline apply to the Raddatz School for the Performing Arts.
3. "You have too much **poten______al** to ignore," Ms. Mooney told Madeline.
4. "The Raddatz School is the finest **institu______on** in this area," she added.
5. "You have such a **spe______al** voice, and the training you would receive could be very **benefi______al** to you if you decided to pursue a singing career."
6. Madeline knew the **competi______on** would be fierce, so she tried not to have **expecta______ons** that were too high.
7. The day of the audition, Madeline took lots of deep breaths and **pa______ently** waited her turn.
8. When she had finished singing, she tried to read the **fa______al** expressions of the admissions panel.
9. They **gra______ously** thanked her and told her that they **appre______ated** her energy and enthusiasm.
10. Two weeks later, when Madeline was starting to have a strong **suspi______on** that she hadn't been accepted, she received her **offi______al** letter.
11. "After all that **specula______on** and worrying about **rejec______on**, it's nice to finally have an answer," Madeline admitted to Ms. Mooney.
12. Her teacher laughed. "This calls for a **celebra______on**!" she exclaimed.

NAME ____________________

Review Digraphs, Silent Consonants, **ti** and **ci**

On the line, write the letter of the word that has the same sound as the digraph of the word in bold.

1. ______ **chocolate** a. Cheryl b. chemistry c. sandwich
2. ______ **otherwise** a. gather b. ruthless c. tollbooth
3. ______ **whittle** a. wheelchair b. whomever c. wholly
4. ______ **physician** a. presume b. foreground c. path
5. ______ **chromosome** a. parchment b. mushroom c. kimono
6. ______ **dwelling** a. dwarf b. anguish c. hallway

Fill in the blank in each sentence below with a word from the box. Underline the silent letter or letters in the word.

lambs	wrinkled	budge	designed	knew	hatched	neighed

1. The sheep and the spring ____________________ trotted across the pasture as the Border collie herded them toward the barn.
2. It was time to milk the goats, but a stubborn female named Christabel refused to ____________________ for Eli.
3. When they heard the clanging of the slop buckets, the pigs immediately ____________________ it was time for breakfast.
4. As he walked across the barnyard, Eli ____________________ his nose and stopped to see if he had stepped in some cow manure.
5. Three chicks had ____________________ early that morning, and the mother hen clucked proudly as she fussed over her new brood.
6. The horses ____________________ and whinnied in their stalls, anxious for their morning feed and a bit of attention.
7. Eli checked the vegetable garden and was satisfied to see that the fence he had ____________________ and built with his father was successful at keeping the animals away.

REVIEW: CHAPTER 1 LESSONS 3–6

NAME ____________________

Review Digraphs, Silent Consonants, **ti** and **ci**

Read the paragraphs below and complete the items that follow.

Chopsticks are eating utensils used in China, Japan, Korea, and Vietnam. They are thought to have been invented in China between three and five thousand years ago and are used as tongs or pincers. They may be made of wood, bamboo, metal, bone, ivory, or even plastic. In Japan, the word *otemoto*, Japanese for *chopstick*, is often written on the wrapper in Japanese characters.

The proper way to hold chopsticks is between the thumb and fingers. The bottom stick stays stationary, while the top stick moves up and down to grasp the food. If the chef has cut the food into small pieces and the rice is sticky enough, eating with chopsticks is simple.

REVIEW: CHAPTER 1 LESSONS 3–6

1. On the lines, write two words that contain the /th/ sound and two that contain the /th/ sound. ____________ ____________

   ____________ ____________

2. On the lines, list three words in which /ch/ makes different sounds.

   ____________ ____________ ____________

3. Underline the four words in the paragraphs that contain silent consonant pairs.
4. Circle all the digraphs in the first paragraph.

Underline the pair of letters that correctly completes each bold word below.

1. Visit Cut 'n' Curl Salon in Linden Shopping Center—our professionally trained **beauti______ans** (ti, ci) will help you look your best!
2. **Atten______on** (ti, ci) pet owners! For one weekend only, bring your dog or cat to Petshop Plus and receive a goodie bag FREE with any purchase.
3. **Men______on** (ti, ci) this ad, and you'll receive $2.00 off the price of admission when you visit the San Francisco Museum of History's **Egyp______an** (ti, ci) exhibit.

NAME ____________________

Lesson 1.7 Vowel Sounds (ai, ay, ei, ey)

The vowel pairs **ai**, **ay**, **ei**, and **ey** can make the long **a** sound, as in *remain*, *hooray*, *reign*, and *prey*.

Read the paragraphs below. Underline the word from the pair in parentheses that has the same long **a** sound as the bold word.

If you like stamps, a collection is fairly easy to establish. Although "**snail-mail**" (weigh, forehead) isn't as popular as it once was, collecting stamps **remains** (habitat, halfway) one of the most popular hobbies **today** (cloak, convey). Buying new stamps and **obtaining** (unlatched, everyday) stamps from other collectors is probably the best way to start.

The first thing to do is decide what focus your collection will have. Will you collect stamps only from **faraway** (veil, transplant) places? Do you have any other interests, like **trains** (mishap, weekday), cats, art, soccer, or **railroad** (disobey, seaweed) souvenirs? Your interests can be a good starting point when choosing a theme for your collection.

Some people collect first-**day** (maintain, caravan) covers, which are envelopes that have stamps attached to them that were canceled on the first day the stamp was issued. Souvenir sheets are also popular. **They** (restrained, healthy) are sheets that have a picture, such as a jungle or an underwater scene, printed on them.

It **may** (upbeat, mermaid) be difficult for a beginner to know how much a stamp is worth. The Internet can be a good source of information. Plenty of sites **explain** (unlatch, swaying) the characteristics that make stamps valuable. If you're **afraid** (reindeer, instead) that you've **overpaid** (approach, hey) for a stamp, it could still be worth researching. Some counterfeit stamps are actually rarer, and so more valuable, than the real stamp they were meant to imitate!

NAME ______________________

Lesson 1.7 Vowel Sounds (ai, ay, ei, ey)

Read the e-mail below. Circle the 16 words that contain the long **a** sound spelled **ai**, **ay**, **ei**, and **ey**. You do not need to mark the same word twice.

From: avmarquez@worldquest.com
Date: May 23, 2008
To: allriledup@techstream.com
Subject: What's up?

Dear Riley,

Are you feeling any better today? It's probably a good thing that you stayed home. Eight other people were absent with the same cold, and Mr. Tanaka made the rest of the class promise we'd do our best to remain healthy.

Ms. Capshaw handed back our essays yesterday. She said I managed to "convey the important points of the argument and convince my audience" of my perspective. Hooray! It's nice to get such praise for a paper that I put so much time and effort into. Did I tell you that I even interviewed my neighbor about his experiences during World War II? I think he'll be quite pleased to see that the details he contributed helped me obtain the results I'd hoped for.

Let me know if you think you'll have recovered enough to meet me at the subway station in the A.M.

Talk to you later!

Alvaro

p.s. Did you fill out the PTA's survey yet? If they receive ninety percent of the surveys by Friday afternoon, they'll pay for a pizza party after the Spring Dance!

NAME ________________________________

Lesson 1.8 Vowel Sounds (ee, ea, ie, ey)

The letters **ee**, **ea**, **ie**, and **ey** can make the long **e** sound you hear in *thirt**ee**n*, *wr**ea**th*, *rel**ie**f*, and *chimn**ey***.

Read each clue. Fill in the letters to complete the word that matches the clue.

1. to promise or make certain	guarant____ ____
2. below	undern____ ____th
3. one part at a time	p____ ____cemeal
4. a mixture or assortment	medl____ ____
5. a type of algae found in the sea	s____ ____w____ ____d
6. to read something and mark errors	proofr____ ____d
7. a person who makes a living sewing	s____ ____mstress

Read the sentences below. Underline the words that contain the long **e** sound spelled **ee**, **ea**, **ie**, and **ey**. You do not need to mark the same word twice.

1. Chimpanzees and other monkeys are frequently the stars of slapstick comedies.

2. *Field of Dreams*, starring Kevin Costner, is a popular movie with baseball fans of all ages.

3. *The Ransom of Red Chief* stars Academy Award nominee Haley Joel Osment.

4. Eddie Murphy provided the voice of the donkey in the animated movie *Shrek*.

5. The canine lead in *Because of Winn-Dixie* is named for the supermarket where he was found.

6. *Cheaper by the Dozen* tells the hilarious story of Mr. and Mrs. Baker raising their enormous brood while trying to fulfill their own dreams, too.

NAME ______________________

Lesson 1.8 Vowel Sounds (**ee**, **ea**, **ie**, **ey**)

Read each sentence and the set of words below it. Underline the word that has the same long **e** sound as the bold word.

1. On a rainy afternoon, **Audrey** and her cousin, Kyle, decided to see if they could find anything interesting in their grandparents' attic.

   lying ordeal healthful

2. Kyle shook out an old blanket that covered a trunk and **sneezed** as a cloud of fine dust surrounded him.

   widespread implement attorney

3. After a few minutes, he **succeeded** in opening the rusty latch on the trunk.

   heartbeat suspend beige

4. **Underneath** a pile of yellowed, brittle napkins, Audrey found some photos.

   suppress dreadful antifreeze

5. In the first one, a dapper gentleman wearing a striped cap and old-fashioned clothes stood with one hand on a **trolley**.

   gymnastics bittersweet stowaway

6. Audrey laughed in **disbelief**. "I had no idea Gramps drove a trolley car!"

   Tennessee nonsense their

7. "Look at this antique **timepiece**," said Kyle, pulling a pocket watch from a cloth-lined box.

   represent kidney freight

8. "It's the same one Gramps is wearing in the photo," Audrey said, **reaching** for the picture.

   dredge stealth parsley

9. "I bet there are **stories** for every photo in that bundle," said Kyle.

   cleave inept forehead

NAME ______________________________

Lesson 1.9 Vowel Sounds (**ind**, **ild**, **igh**)

The vowel **i** can make a long sound when followed by **nd**, **ld**, or **gh**, as in *beh**ind***, *m**ild***, and *day**ligh**t*.

Read the clues below. Choose the word from the box that matches each clue, and write it in the numbered space in the crossword puzzle.

rind	mild	mastermind	hindsight	copyright
wild	slight	colorblind	frightened	

Across

1. legal protection for a creative work, like a book or play
3. small in size or amount
4. moderate; not extreme
6. an antonym for *tame*
7. scared; having fear
8. a person who directs a project

Down

1. unable to see certain colors
2. a clear view or understanding of a situation after it has occurred
5. the tough outer covering of a fruit

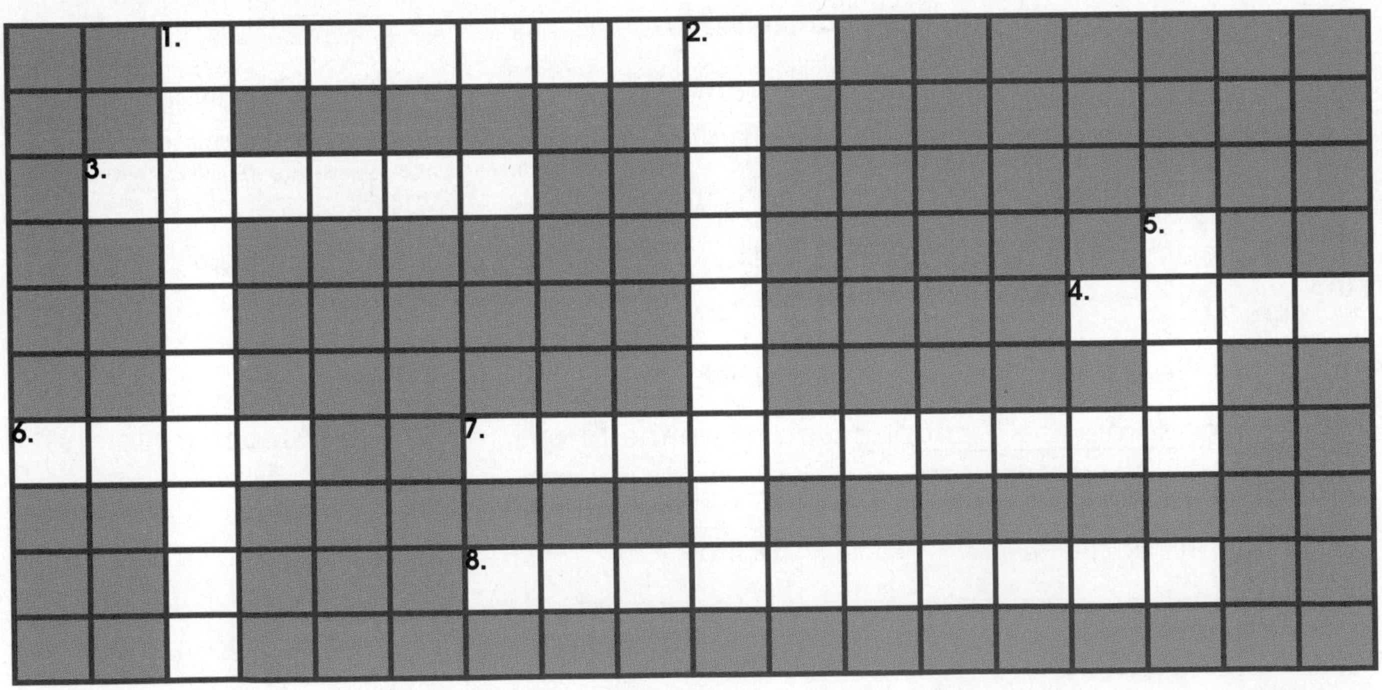

NAME ______________________________

Lesson 1.9 Vowel Sounds (**ind**, **ild**, **igh**)

Read the words below. Circle the letter of the word or words in each set that have a long **i** sound.

1. a. transmit	**b.** blight	**c.** yield	**d.** mildest
2. a. childish	**b.** birthright	**c.** humankind	**d.** handkerchief
3. a. behind	**b.** hardship	**c.** obtain	**d.** overnight
4. a. collies	**b.** bullfight	**c.** imprint	**d.** flinching
5. a. childhood	**b.** squid	**c.** outright	**d.** battleship

Write the words that contain the long **i** sound spelled **igh**, **ind**, and **ild** beside the correct headings. You do not need to list the same word more than once.

A mural is a painting done on a wall or a ceiling. Murals can have many purposes. In a home, a mural may be purely decorative. For example, on the wall of a child's room an artist might create a nighttime scene, complete with nocturnal creatures, constellations, and silvery moonlight.

Murals in public places often carry messages. They may serve as reminders of important issues, like the plight of the poor or racial inequality. Since the 1970s, more than 2,000 murals have been made in the public spaces of Northern Ireland. Most give insight into the political beliefs of the residents.

Murals frequently decorate walls or the sides of buildings in urban areas. Sometimes they are created by a group of students with the help of a local artist. The colors are wild, and the paintings give life and energy to the city. It's a delightful surprise, when pausing at a street corner or a stoplight, to find a story unfolding across the side of a neighborhood school or bookstore.

igh: ______________ ______________ ______________

______________ ______________ ______________

____

ind: ______________ ______________

ild: ______________ ______________

NAME ______________________

Lesson 1.10 Vowel Sounds (**oa**, **ow**, **old**, **oll**, **ost**)

- The letters **oa** and **ow** can make the long **o** sound as in *t**oa**d* and *kn**ow**n*.
- The vowel **o** can make a long sound when followed by **ld**, **ll**, and **st**, as in *f**old***, *r**oll**ing*, and *m**ost***.

Read each clue below. The word that matches the clue is written in bold beside it, but the letters are scrambled. Unscramble the letters and write the word on the line. Each word will contain a long vowel combination from above.

1. a fungus that forms on rotten food **odml** ____________
2. to become too big for something, like clothes **oouwgrt** ____________
3. a fee charged for using a road or bridge **ltol** ____________
4. an antonym for *least* **omts** ____________
5. black briquettes used to start a fire in a grill **arcchola** ____________
6. material used to cover a person's eyes and prevent him or her from seeing **inblldd fo** ____________
7. a figure intended to frighten birds away from a farmer's crops **ecrsarcow** ____________
8. to criticize or speak angrily to **solcd** ____________
9. a person who receives guests **thso** ____________
10. to talk about oneself with a lot of pride **bosta** ____________
11. to move up and down a computer screen **roscll** ____________
12. a bright warm light without a flame **wgol** ____________
13. a place where two roads intersect **oscrsrdsoa** ____________
14. to take a leisurely walk **rolstl** ____________
15. another word for *wallet* **llfobild** ____________
16. the sound a frog makes **ackro** ____________
17. a synonym for *nearly* **osaltm** ____________

NAME ______________________________

Lesson 1.10 Vowel Sounds (**oa**, **ow**, **old**, **oll**, **ost**)

Read the paragraphs below. Complete each word with the correct letter combination (**oa**, **ow**, **oll**, **old**, or **ost**).

My trip began when I was orphaned at the age of 12. It quickly became clear that I would have to make my ______**n** way in the world. There was work to be had at the docks, and for several days I toiled, **unl**______**ding** goods from cargo ships that arrived from exotic ports around the world.

On my third day at the docks, I was **appr**______**ched** by an imposing man wearing a charcoal-gray **cl**______**k** and a fine silken scarf wrapped around his **thr**______**t**. If only I had **kn**______**n** what tragedies I would **beh**______ in my travels with Captain Cobb.

My first few days were uneventful. Then, things suddenly changed. The weather turned **c**______, and I wrapped my thin **c**______**t** more tightly around my body. As I **str**______**ed** toward the warm, **gl**______**ing** embers in the wood stove, I heard the sounds of arguing drifting up from **bel**______ deck.

I tried to **h**______ my breath as I crept closer to the voices. Parts of the conversation disappeared in the **bl**______**ing** winds, but I clearly heard words like *treasure*, *gold*, **blindf**______, *takeover*, and *prisoner*. It was obvious to me now that I had **unkn**______**ingly** cast my lot with a band of pirates. Then and there, I **b**______**ly** decided to plan my escape. I took note of where the **r**______**boat** was stored and carefully began **st**______**ing** away food from every meal.

The day of my escape dawned gray and stormy. I **sl**______**ly** and quietly **l**______**ered** my rickety boat. As it touched the water, I heard a sinister chuckle and knew I would not be leaving that day.

NAME ______________________

Review Vowel Sounds

Read the recipe below. Underline the letter combination from the pair in parentheses to correctly complete each bold word.

Southwestern Salad

1 each, **sw_____t** (ea, ee) red pepper and **gr_____n** (ee, ie) pepper

2 tomatoes

1 15-ounce can each black **b_____ns** (ea, ee) and corn

1 pound ground **turk_____** (ey, ay)

4 ounces **l_____t** (igh, ild) sour cream

1 package taco **s_____soning** (ie, ea), spicy or **m_____** (ild, ind)

3 tablespoons of chopped **parsl_____** (ai, ey)

2 cups cooked pasta, such as macaroni or farfalle

1 cup **l_____**-fat (ow, oa) shredded cheddar **ch_____se** (ee, ea)

- With the help of an adult, cook the ground turkey in a saucepan **c_____ted** (ow, oa) with cooking **spr_____** (ay, ey) .
- While you are waiting for the **m_____t** (ee, ea) to cook, dice the peppers and tomatoes, and place them in a large mixing **b_____l** (ow, oa). Rinse and **dr_____n** (ay, ai) the beans and corn, and add them to the bowl.
- When the turkey is done, remove it from the **h_____t** (ea, ee).
- **M_____nwhile** (ie, ea), add the taco seasoning, and parsley to the sour **cr_____m** (ei, ea) and stir thoroughly. Add the sour cream mixture, turkey, and pasta to the bowl with the vegetables. Stir until blended.
- Chill the salad in the refrigerator until it is **c_____** (old, ost). **L_____d** (oa, ow) **_____ch** (ee, ea) serving with two tablespoons of cheese.
- Serve with dinner **r_____s** (oll, oa), tortillas, or nacho chips.

NAME ______________________________

Review Vowel Sounds

Read the sets of words below. Circle the two words in each set that have the same long vowel sound.

1.	sustain	sunbeam	**4.**	oversleep	beige
	afloat	convey		attorney	letterhead
2.	uptight	unwinding	**5.**	progress	enrolled
	slingshot	swimming		suspense	sugarcoat
3.	roaming	couch	**6.**	breaded	decay
	withhold	trough		reins	gazelle

Read each sentence below. On the line, write the long vowel sound you hear in each bold word. If a word contains more than one long vowel sound, separate the two sounds with a slash. (Ex.: long **i**/long **a**)

1. Although the red-**bellied** ________________ woodpecker has a small patch of color on its belly, the bird's **bright** ________________ red head is much harder to miss.
2. The **snow** ________________ goose is **mostly** ________________ white, but a less common **grayish**- blue ________________ variety also exists.
3. Unlike other herons, the **green** ________________ heron has a very short, stocky neck.
4. The common **yellowthroat** ________________, which lives in **fields** ________________ and marshes, has a very distinctive song: *witchity-witchity-witchity-witchity.*
5. The brown-headed cowbird is a parasitic bird, which means that it **lays** ________________ its eggs in a **host** ________________ bird's nest and **leaves** ________________ the babies for the other bird to **raise** ________________.
6. The **chimney** ________________ swift, one of the fastest flying birds, spends **almost** ________________ all its time in the air and is rarely seen perching or on the ground.

REVIEW: CHAPTER 1 LESSONS 7-10

NAME ______________________________

Lesson 1.11 Vowel Sounds (oo, ew, ou, ui, ue)

- The letters **oo**, **ew**, **ou**, **ui**, and **ue** can make the /ü/ sound, as in *upr**oo**t*, *withdr**ew***, *regr**ou**p*, *cr**ui**se*, and *tr**ue***.
- The letters **oo** can also make the /ù/ sound you hear in *sh**oo**k*.

Read the definitions below. For each word in column 2, underline the letters that make the /ü/ sound and circle the letters that make the /ù/ sound. On the line, write the letter of the word that matches each definition.

1. ______	the act of chasing something in order to catch it	**a.** nuisance
2. ______	occurring later than planned or scheduled	**b.** pursuit
3. ______	not wearing shoes	**c.** livelihood
4. ______	an annoyance	**d.** nook
5. ______	the means by which a person earns a living	**e.** overdue
6. ______	a small, cozy, or hidden area	**f.** barefoot

Read each sentence below. Underline the word from the pair in parentheses that has the same /ü/ or /ù/ vowel sound as the word in bold.

1. On Saturday night, a large **group** (sour, papoose) of friends and relatives will meet at Clausen Beach for their annual clambake.
2. Mr. Krauss **recruits** (booth, checkbook) as many people as he can to help shuck the corn and rinse the clams in saltwater.
3. The youngest kids eagerly scour the beach for pieces of **driftwood** (platoon, could) that are **suitable** (handbook, curlicue) for the bonfire.
4. As the sun disappears below the horizon, the **moonlight** (fatherhood, revenue) fills the beach with a silvery glow.
5. Although everyone is a bit more **subdued** (cruising, clucked) than when the evening began, the mention of dessert infuses the group with energy.

NAME ______________________________

Lesson 1.11 Vowel Sounds (**oo**, **ew**, **ou**, **ui**, **ue**)

Read the review below. Complete each word with the correct letter combination (**oo**, **ew**, **ou**, **ui**, or **ue**).

B_____k Review of *By the Light of the* ***M_____n*** by Cameron Rickman

After reading Cameron Rickman's 2006 novel, *By the Light of the Moon*, there is no doubt in my mind why it was one of the nominees for the **N_____bery** Award. Having read two of Rickman's other books for youth, I **kn_____** that this book was likely to have strong characters and an unusual, interesting plot. I was not disappointed.

The story opens in an airport on a **gl_____my aftern_____n** in May. The reader quickly learns that Anna, the protagonist, was adopted in early **childh_____d**. The author does an excellent job of creating suspense at the beginning of the novel. A mystery surrounds Anna's past, so she decides to **purs_____** the **tr_____** story of her biological family. Anna and her adoptive father are en **r_____te** to Thailand, where Anna was born. But why is Mr. Haviland so strongly against Anna's **purs_____t** of her past? As they sit in the airport surrounded by **s_____tcases**, the air between them is filled with tension.

Rickman continues to build tension **thr_____ghout** the book. He drops **cl_____s** for the reader, but they are few and far between. He relies on the reader's intelligence and close attention to keep up with the adventures.

I believe this book is **s_____table** for readers over ten years old. It deals with some difficult issues, like **parenth_____d**, adoption, truth, and trust. The characters have many layers, just like real people do. I would give this book four stars—my highest rating.

NAME ______________________________

Lesson 1.12 Vowel Sounds (**au**, **aw**, **al**, **alk**, **all**)

- The vowel pairs **au** and **aw** can make the same sound, as in *t**au**ght* and *sees**aw***.
- When the vowel **a** is followed by **l**, **lk**, or **ll**, as in *m**al**t*, *st**alk***, or *inst**all***, it makes the same sound as **au** and **aw** do.

Read the sentences below. Circle the 14 words that contain the /ô/ sound spelled **au**, **aw**, **al**, **all**, or **alk**. You do not need to mark the same word twice.

1. Although many people think of fairy tales as reading material for children, they were first intended for an audience of all ages.
2. Some tales had a known author, like the Brothers Grimm, while other anonymous stories were passed down generation after generation.
3. Fairy tales of long ago often had sad endings in which awful things happened to the characters.
4. This was because some tales were meant to caution people against behaviors that could be dangerous or unwise.
5. Modern versions of fairy tales are drawn with more cheerful pictures and happier endings.
6. *Cinderella*, *Hansel and Gretel*, *Sleeping Beauty*, *Little Red Riding Hood*, and *Jack and the Beanstalk* are among the most well-known fairy tales.
7. There are few people who are unfamiliar with the little red-hooded granddaughter who travels through the woods to visit her grandma and narrowly avoids being caught by the wolf.
8. Part of the appeal of fairy tales is that the smaller, weaker underdog is often able to outsmart someone older, wiser, or brawnier.
9. Throughout the centuries, fairy tales have taught countless lessons and entertained people with their timeless, imaginative characters.

NAME ______________________________

Lesson 1.12 Vowel Sounds (**au**, **aw**, **al**, **alk**, **all**)

Read the following sentences. The bold word in each sentence is scrambled. Rearrange the letters to form a word that contains **au**, **aw**, **al**, **alk**, or **all**, and write it on the line.

1. Six months ago, Mr. Trasco stood at the **bradlackoh** ____________________ writing down our ideas.
2. "If we don't raise some extra money, programs like **labbastelk** ____________________ and choir will have to be canceled," he announced.
3. At the end of class, we voted on the best idea among the ones **drawscle** ____________________ across the board.
4. The day of the carnival finally arrived, and booths filled with different activities lined the edges of the school's **shaltap** ____________________ parking lot.
5. The crowds were so huge that police officers were hired to stop traffic whenever people needed to use the **scrowskal** ____________________ in front of the school.
6. A dunking booth was **edtinsall** ____________________ near the entrance, and our principal, Mrs. Young, volunteered to be the first "victim."

Read each clue. Fill in the letters to complete the word that matches the clue.

1. imperfect	fl____ ____ed
2. captivated; unable to look away	enthr____ ____ ____ed
3. extremely upset	distr____ ____ght
4. a stem of a plant	st____ ____ ____
5. a short, pleasurable trip	j____ ____nt
6. spreading out in a disorderly way	spr____ ____ling

NAME ______________________

Lesson 1.13 Vowel Diphthongs

When two vowel sounds come together and create a new sound, the combination they form is called a **diphthong** (*dip thông*).
- The diphthongs **oi**, as in *m**oi**st*, and **oy**, as in ***oy**ster*, make the same sound.

Read each description below. Choose the word from the box that matches the clue. Write it on the line, and circle the diphthong.

joyfulness	employer	annoy	viewpoint	loyalty	Des Moines	hoist

1. I am a company or person for whom others work. Some might call me the boss. ______________
2. I am a verb that means to *lift* or *pull up*. You could use me in this sentence: *The girls helped their dad _____ the sails.* ______________
3. The word *faithfulness* is a synonym for me. I describe a quality that good friends or family members show for one another. ______________
4. Founded in 1843, I am Iowa's capital city. ______________
5. I am a feeling of great happiness or pleasure. ______________
6. I am another word for *bother* or *irritate*. ______________
7. I am a person's perspective or the way he or she sees things. ______________

Read the headlines below. Underline the word from the pair in parentheses that has the same vowel sound as the bold word or words.

1. Adventurer Begins **Voyage** Around the World—by Balloon!
   (Moscow, toil)
2. Fans **Disappointed** When Singer Jett Mullin Cancels World Tour
   (rebound, convoy)
3. Hurricane Chloe **Destroys** 42 Homes Along Florida Coast
   (prowl, moisture)
4. Britain's **Royal** Family to Visit the States and Meet with President
   (spoiled, moan)

NAME ______________________

Lesson 1.13 Vowel Diphthongs

- The diphthongs **ou**, as in *try**out***, and **ow**, as in ***tow**n*, make the same sound.

Read the paragraphs below. Underline the eight words that contain the /ou/ sound spelled **ou**. Circle the seven words that contain the /ou/ sound spelled **ow**. You do not need to mark the same word more than once.

What kinds of things do you read on the computer? Have you ever tried reading an e-book, or electronic book? What about a newspaper article or your favorite magazine? For many people, it's difficult to spend long amounts of time in front of a computer screen. They would rather find a more comfortable place in the house to read, like a cozy chair or the couch. A laptop computer is portable, but it is still bulkier than a magazine or small book. It's also hard for someone reading in a car or outdoors to see the screen in bright light.

Several renowned companies on the cutting edge of technology are now working on some ideas that would forever change the way people read. How does the idea of electronic paper sound to you? It's difficult to explain exactly how this concept works. The basic idea, though, is that the battery-powered paper is filled with tiny capsules. Each capsule contains black and white particles that carry an electric charge. Using the electricity in each capsule, a computer program determines whether the black or white particles are allowed to come to the surface of the paper. The black particles form patterns that create letters, symbols, and words. When you "turn the page," different particles rise to the surface and form the words and pictures on the next page of the book or magazine.

Although it seems like something that might be found in a science fiction novel, it's possible that in the future a single piece of electronic paper could somehow hold the contents of an entire book. The countdown to the books of the future has begun.

NAME ____________________

Review Vowel Sounds and Diphthongs

Read the clues below. On the line, write the word from the box that matches the clue and has the sound listed in parentheses. Then, find each word in the word search puzzle. Words may be written forward, backward, or diagonally.

squall	oyster	compound	true	scowl	shook	awkward	whirlpool	suitable	rejoice

1. a word that is made of two shorter words (/ou/) ____________
2. to celebrate with great happiness (/oi/) ____________
3. a current of water that rotates very quickly (/ü/) ____________
4. appropriate (/ü/) ____________
5. clumsy; not graceful (/ô/) ____________
6. the past tense of the verb *shake* (/u̇/) ____________
7. to glare or frown (/ou/) ____________
8. a short, violent storm with wind and rain or snow (/ô/) ____________
9. an edible shellfish that sometimes contains pearls (/oi/) ____________
10. not false (/ü/) ____________

f	a	h	m	s	d	g	i	o	e	b	c	a	a
j	w	j	r	t	q	l	l	a	u	q	s	b	n
w	k	h	v	c	r	w	u	l	l	v	u	f	r
n	w	x	i	c	e	o	t	y	h	s	i	s	u
r	a	b	d	r	h	c	a	i	m	k	t	f	z
e	r	k	r	q	l	s	o	o	v	d	a	h	r
j	d	h	j	b	s	p	i	k	c	z	b	p	e
o	m	m	r	w	h	n	o	g	i	l	l	d	t
i	e	d	n	u	o	p	m	o	c	f	e	n	s
c	h	j	m	a	o	c	t	u	l	s	w	b	y
e	n	m	p	l	k	r	e	t	r	u	e	q	o

REVIEW: CHAPTER 1 LESSONS 11–13

NAME ______________________

Review Vowel Sounds and Diphthongs

Read the paragraphs below. Underline the letter combination in parentheses that shares a vowel sound found in the bold word.

When people think of **baseball** (au, oa), the legendary hitter Babe Ruth is often the first player to come to mind. By most **accounts** (oi, ow), he is the greatest athlete in the history of the game. Ruth was one of the first five players elected to the Baseball **Hall** (aw, ou) of Fame. Today, his **autograph** (all, ou) can be worth **thousands** (ow, ui) of dollars. His fame helped baseball **zoom** (ue, oy) to **new** (ow, oo) heights of popularity during the 1920s and 30s. The fans that turned **out** (ow, au) to watch the Bambino play were rarely **disappointed** (ou, oy) by the performance they **saw** (au, ou).

Babe Ruth, born George Herman Ruth in 1895, was known for being mischievous as a **boy** (ew, oi). Because his parents were concerned **about** (ow, oo) his behavior, they sent him to a strict **school** (aw, ue). It was there that young George was **taught** (all, ou) the ins and outs of baseball and developed a great **enjoyment** (oi, ow) for playing the game.

In 1914, Ruth was **recruited** (ew, oi) to **join** (ou, oy) the minor league Baltimore Orioles. During the next few years, he played for the Boston Red Sox where he excelled as a pitcher. By 1917, he began pitching less and spending more time in the **outfield** (ow, ui). He **soon** (oy, ew) surprised many people when he proved he was **also** (all, ou) talented as a hitter and outfielder.

After several years, Ruth was traded to the New York Yankees. During his first year in New York, Ruth hit 54 home runs, breaking his record of 29 home runs in a season. Throughout his career with the Yankees, Ruth continued to set records and **astound** (ow, aw) people with his talent.

People **around** (ue, ow) the world mourned Ruth's loss when he died in 1948, but they were grateful for **all** (au, ou) that he had given to America's favorite sport.

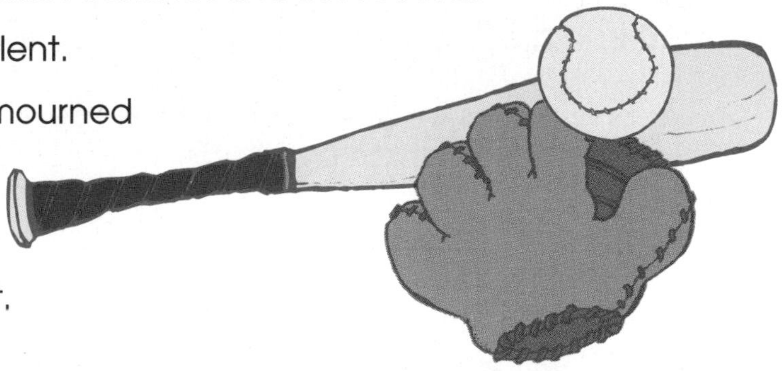

NAME ______________________________

Lesson 1.14 The Schwa Sound

The **schwa sound**, represented by the symbol **ə**, is the /uh/ sound you hear at the beginning of the word *allow*.

- The vowels **a**, **e**, **i**, **o**, and **u** can all make the schwa sound, as in ***a**round*, *barr**e**l*, *penc**i**l*, *maj**o**r*, and *cact**u**s*.
- Sometimes, vowel pairs can also make the schwa sound, as in *relat**io**n* and *caut**iou**s*.

Read each group of words below. Circle the word in each group that contains the schwa sound. Use a dictionary if you need help with pronunciation.

1. limber	recede	catch
2. pause	dispel	cardinal
3. graphic	scallop	wheezing
4. passion	passage	bypass
5. dairy	diary	radar

On the line, rewrite each bold word below using the symbol for a schwa (ə) in place of the letter or letters that make the schwa sound.

1. My friend took second place in the **regional** spelling bee. ______________

2. The fresh **aroma** of baked bread drifted from the kitchen. ______________

3. With each tug of the rope and swing of the axe, the **mountaineer** inched her way slowly toward the summit. ______________

4. A **floral** bouquet was placed at the center of each table at the reception. ______________

5. Malia's **ancestors** came to Hawaii hundreds of years ago. ______________

6. The **koala** slowly ate eucalyptus leaves. ______________

7. No one knows for sure how many people it took to build the Egyptian **pyramids**. ______________

NAME ____________________

Lesson 1.14 The Schwa Sound

Read the following paragraphs. For each word in bold, circle the vowel or vowels that make the schwa sound.

Throughout history, our **nation** and its **citizens** have had to endure a number of difficult and trying **moments**. Few events were as sad as the **assassinations** of presidents Abraham Lincoln and John F. Kennedy. Although they are not discussed as **often**, the deaths of James Garfield and William McKinley were equally shocking to the **Americans** of their time.

President James Garfield took office on March 4, 1881. Only four months **later**, on July 2, Garfield was walking through a Washington, D.C., railroad station when Charles J. Guiteau shot him. Garfield lived for **another** 80 days, but **medical** knowledge during that time was limited. On **September** 19, President Garfield passed **away**. He had been president for only six and a half months.

President William McKinley began his **second** term in March 1901. Due to America's **victory** in the Spanish-American War, McKinley had **easily** defeated William Jennings Bryan in the **previous** fall's election. In September 1901, McKinley **traveled** to Buffalo, New York, to give a speech at the Pan-American **Exposition**. It was at this World's Fair that tragedy would strike.

On September 6, McKinley stood at the front of a line of people waiting to shake the president's hand. Slowly, Leon Czolgosz made his way through the line. Czolgosz was an **anarchist**—someone who believes that all forms of government are bad and should be **abolished**. Although many anarchists were **peaceful**, others **performed violent** acts.

When Czolgosz reached the front of the line, he shot McKinley and was immediately **taken** into custody. McKinley was rushed to the **hospital** in an **ambulance**, making him the first president to ride in an **automobile**. Sadly, McKinley died of his wounds eight days later.

NAME ______________________

Lesson 1.14 The Schwa Sound

Many words that end in a consonant plus **le**, **al**, or **el** contain the schwa sound.

rumble (rumbəl)   vocal (vocəl)   label (labəl)

Read the sentences below. In some of the words, the schwa symbol (ə) has replaced vowels that make the schwa sound. On the line, rewrite these words with their correct spellings.

1. The **tropicəl** ________________ Amazonian rain forest stretches across more than a billion acres of land.
2. More than two million species of insects and two thousand types of birds and **mamməls** ________________ live in the region.
3. **Environmentəl** ________________ groups around the world are working to protect the Amazon rain forest, a fifth of which has already been lost.
4. **Locəl** ________________ species of plants and **animəls** ________________ that do not exist anywhere else in the world are in danger of becoming extinct.
5. The Amazon is shared by nine South American countries that benefit from the **materiəls** ________________ the forest produces, as well as from the tourists who **travəl** ________________ to see this place of great beauty.
6. Some conservation programs allow **peopəl** ________________ to buy an acre of **jungəl** ________________ land in order to keep it safe from harm.
7. Six-foot-wide water lilies with thin, delicate **petəls** ________________ can be found floating along the lakes and rivers of the Amazon.
8. The tapir, which looks like some sort of prehistoric animal, has a nose that **resembəls** ________________ an elephant's trunk.
9. Although the anaconda is not poisonous, its large size and strong **muscəls** ________________ allow it to **tackəl** ________________ and feed on creatures as large as cows.

NAME ______________________

Lesson 1.14 The Schwa Sound

The **schwa sound** occurs in unstressed syllables. For example, in the word *ba′· sin* the first syllable is stressed. The second syllable contains the schwa sound.

In the following words, the vowel that makes the /ə/ sound is set in bold. Notice how it appears only in unstressed syllables.

en′·**e**·my c**a**s·sette′ nui′·s**a**nce ser′·m**o**n p**a**·go′·d**a**

Read each definition and the pronunciation beside it. On the line, write the word.

1. a tradition or habit cus′·təm ______________
2. materials made of baked clay cə·ram′·ics ______________
3. relating to mail service or post offices po′·stəl ______________
4. a person who travels in outer space as′·trə·not′ ______________
5. a married male hus′·bənd ______________

Read the sentences below. Underline the stressed syllable or syllables in each bold word, and circle the vowel or vowels that make the schwa sound.

1. In 1910, Robert Baden-Powell founded the Girl Guides of Great Britain as a **coun·ter·part** to the group for boys he began in 1908.
2. In 1912, Juliette Low started the Girl Scouts, a **sim·i·lar** organization in the United States.
3. The Girl Scouts and Girl Guides both **fo·cus** on leadership, **char·ac·ter**, community, outdoor activities, and service.
4. In **A·mer·i·ca**, the five age groups are called the *Daisies, Brownies, Juniors,* ***Ca·dettes***, and *Seniors.*
5. Today, there are nearly 10 **mil·lion** members in 144 countries.

NAME ________________________

Lesson 1.15 The Sounds of y

- The letter **y** can make the /y/ sound you hear in ***y**ounger*.
- It can make the long **i** sound, as in *h**y**ena* and *sl**y***.
- The letter **y** can make the long **e** sound, as in *trick**y***.
- In the middle of a word, **y** can make the short **i** sound, as in *m**y**th*.

Read each sentence. Circle the word below the sentence that has the same sound of **y** as the bold word.

1. The yak is a member of the bovine **family**, as are bison and cattle.

   yacht policy python mysterious

2. **Yaks** are found in Tibet and mountainous areas of central Asia.

   Egypt occupy geometry yonder

3. **Typical** uses for yaks include milk, meat, cheese, and fiber.

   petrifying yesterday rhythm yowled

4. The yak's soft, **shaggy** fur can be turned into yarn.

   pastry nylon Plymouth barnyard

5. The yak's fur coat can keep it warm and **dry**, even at temperatures as low as 40 degrees below zero.

   yanked pygmy firefly dictionary

6. Yaks are often used as pack animals and can transport **heavy** loads through the mountains.

   cycle gymnasium yodel enemy

7. Trees are scarce in parts of Tibet, so dried yak dung is a useful **type** of fuel.

   yolk crypt angrily myself

8. Yaks have more red blood cells than cattle do, which helps them better absorb **oxygen** from the thin mountain air.

   yeast mythical horrify extremely

NAME ______________________________

Lesson 1.15 The Sounds of y

Read the sentences below. On the line beside each bold word, write the sound **y** makes in the word (long **i**, short **i**, **y**, or long **e**). Hint: Some words may contain more than one sound of **y**.

1. Sanjana has been told **repeatedly** ________________ that she is **musically** ________________ inclined, so she is **applying** ________________ to the famous Juilliard School in New **York** ________________ City.
2. Thirteen-**year**-old ________________ Ramon, who is going to become a stunt double someday, has already been **skydiving** ________________, parasailing, and bungee jumping.
3. When Jenna graduates from the International **Culinary** ________________ Institute, she plans to open a **bakery** ________________ in **Yorkshire** ________________, England.
4. **Kyle** ________________ reads **approximately** ________________ two **mystery** ________________ novels a week and has nearly completed writing the first mystery book of his career.
5. Dana has a small **chemistry** ________________ lab set up in one corner of her bedroom, but she longs for the day when she'll have access to a real **laboratory** ________________.

Read the sets of words below. Circle the two words in each set in which **y** makes the same sound.

1.	anchovy	nymph	5.	gypped	backyard
	amplifying	icy		defy	yield
2.	hyphen	yesterday	6.	shyest	everything
	physician	Olympian		financially	yours
3.	spying	hieroglyphics	7.	particularly	yellow-jacket
	youth	magnify		hyena	dying
4.	rhyming	years	8.	yonder	ladybug
	stingy	yucca		canyon	mysterious

NAME ______________________________

Lesson 1.16 R-Controlled Vowels (**ar**, **er**, **ir**, **or**, **ur**)

When the letter **r** follows a vowel, it changes the vowel's sound.
- The letters **ar** make the sound you hear in *reg**ar**d*.
- The letters **or** make the sound you hear in *th**or**n*.
- The letters **er**, **ir**, and **ur** make the same sound, as in *n**er**ve*, *tw**ir**l*, and ***ur**ge*.

Read the titles and author names in the list below. Circle each word that contains an **r**-controlled vowel.

Ms. Alvarez's 6th Grade Reading List

- *Red Scarf Girl* by Ji-Li Jiang
- *Monster* by Walter Dean Myers
- *North to Freedom* by Anne Holm
- *The Watsons Go to Birmingham—1963* by Christopher Paul Curtis
- *The True Confessions of Charlotte Doyle* by Avi
- *Summer of My German Soldier* by Bette Green
- *Morning Girl* by Michael Dorris
- *The Iceberg Hermit* by Arthur Roth
- *M. C. Higgins the Great* by Virginia Hamilton
- *House of Sports* by M. Russo
- *Ninjas, Piranhas, and Galileo* by Greg Leitich Smith
- *The Borning Room* by Paul Fleischman
- *The Secret Garden* by Frances Hodgson Burnett
- *Island (Survival, Book Two)* by Gordon Korman

On the lines below, write a book title and author for each **r**-controlled vowel sound. You can find the names and titles at a library or in an online catalog.

ar: ______________________________

er: ______________________________

ur: ______________________________

NAME ______________________

Lesson 1.16 R-Controlled Vowels (ar, er, ir, or, ur)

Read the diary entry below. Underline the word from the pair in parentheses that has the same **r**-controlled vowel sound as the bold word.

Dear Diary,

The last couple of weeks have been among the most ***interesting*** *(smirk, coastguard) of my life. I can't believe how much I've learned in such a* ***short*** *(converge, seashore) time. My family arrived at Camp Frontier* ***unsure*** *(leotard, swerve) of what to expect. We knew that we would be taught some* ***nature*** *(mirth, uniform) and* ***survival*** *(midterm, hornet) skills. I was also eager to learn how past* ***generations*** *(guitar, sunburn) lived off the land.*

Last week, we ***harvested*** *(bizarre, nervous) vegetables and berries from the* ***garden*** *(blurt, lifeguard). Cassie and I spent all day in the hot kitchen canning and* ***preserving*** *(lurking, junkyard) everything so that we would have enough provisions for the coming* ***winter*** *(distort, emerge). It was steamy, tedious work, but in the end, we had* ***jar*** *(bookmark, concerned) after jar of blackberry jam, peaches, beans, tomatoes, and* ***peppers*** *(transform, purse).*

I've also milked the cows and goats in the barn every ***morning*** *(purge, carnivore) just after sunrise. I've* ***churned*** *(adverb, bombard) butter by hand from the cows' sweet cream, I can start a fire with a piece of flint and some twigs, and I can identify at least 15* ***birds*** *(suburb, newborn) just by hearing their calls. Not too bad for a city* ***girl*** *(splurge, charming), huh?*

I've met people from all over the country—everywhere from ***Oregon*** *(trademark, affordable) to* ***Arkansas*** *(squirted, postmark) to* ***Vermont*** *(passport, quirky). We've all learned so much from* ***observing*** *(thirst, Denmark) each other. I feel like a strong community has been* ***formed*** *(nurse, discord) here. It will feel strange to* ***return*** *(proverb, lard) to* ***modern*** *(scorch, whirl) life, but I know that we'll take with us all the skills we've learned.*

NAME ______________________________

Lesson 1.17 More r-Controlled Vowels (air, are, ear, eer)

- The letters **air** and **are** can make the same sound, as in *rep**air*** and *prep**are***.
- The letters **ear** and **eer** can make the same sound, as in *app**ear*** and *st**eer***. The letters **ear** can also make the sound you hear in *sw**ear***.

Read the definitions below. On the line, write the word from the box that matches each definition, and circle the **r**-controlled vowel letter combination.

smear	solitaire	gear	beware	questionnaire	rare	steer	volunteer

1. a person who offers to do something, often for free ______________
2. a list of questions used for gathering information ______________
3. to guide a vehicle using a wheel ______________
4. not common; something that doesn't occur often ______________
5. to spread a sticky or greasy material ______________
6. a game of cards one plays alone ______________
7. equipment ______________
8. to be cautious of something ______________

Read each sentence below. On the line, write the letter combination (**air**, **are**, **eer**, or **ear**) that correctly completes each bold word.

1. Bill Gates is the owner of the largest **softw**__________ company in the world.
2. Not only is he a **billion**__________**e**, but he is also the richest person in the world.
3. Even at a young age, Gates had a **fl**__________ for math and science.
4. Throughout his **car**__________, Gates has had many challenges.
5. Bill Gates and his wife, Melinda, are **aw**__________ of how fortunate they are, so each **y**__________ they **sh**__________ their wealth by donating millions of dollars to charity.

NAME ____________________

Lesson 1.17 More r-Controlled Vowels (air, are, ear, eer)

Read the sentences below. Underline the word from the pair in parentheses that has the same **r**-controlled vowel sound as the bold word beside it.

1. It is **unclear** (swear, disappear) exactly how Ask a Stupid Question Day started, but it was probably begun by teachers who wanted students to feel comfortable asking anything.
2. Evoloterra, celebrated on July 20, marks the day when human beings first **dared** (millionaire, speared) to land on the moon.
3. April 1, also known as April Fools' Day, is a day to **beware** (reindeer, solitaire) of any tricksters you might know.
4. Have you ever heard of National Catfish Day? It has been celebrated on June 25 every **year** (career, pears) since 1987.
5. October 15, White Cane Safety Day, celebrates the achievements of people who are visually **impaired** (shear, wearable).
6. Wright Brothers' Day commemorates the **fearless** (outerwear, auctioneer) first flight of Wilbur and Orville Wright on December 17, 1903.
7. Boxing Day, celebrated in Britain on December 26, is often marked by **volunteers** (smeared, wheelchair) who donate gifts or money to charities.
8. Earth Day, celebrated on April 22, helps bring **awareness** (bear, Shakespeare) to important environmental issues.

Read each set of words below. Underline the word that has a different **r**-controlled vowel sound than the rest of the words in the set.

1. fairly	clearing	musketeer	appearance
2. questionnaire	underwear	nearly	despair
3. warfare	peer	affair	wearing
4. threadbare	spearhead	engineering	steer
5. snare	millionaire	nightmare	dearest

NAME ____________________

Review Schwa, the Sounds of y, and r-controlled Vowels

For each bold word, underline the stressed syllable, and circle the vowel or vowels that make the schwa sound.

Too many **an·i·mals** in the world don't have a place to call home or **peo·ple** to protect them. **Thou·sands** of these animals get a **sec·ond** chance at a **spec·ial** place called Best Friends Animal Sanctuary, located in Kanab, Utah. The motto of Best Friends is "No more homeless pets."

Today, more than 1,500 animals live at the sanctuary. There are plenty of **com·mon** house pets, like cats and dogs, but Best Friends is also home to horses, pigs, goats, owls, rabbits, and **doz·ens** of other **va·ri·e·ties** of critters. Some are sick, and many were **a·ban·doned** or **a·bused**. Best Friends **wel·comes** all animals, regardless of their history. Once an animal enters the sanctuary, it will be treated with kindness and respect. Hundreds of animals find good homes through the **ef·forts** of Best Friends. The animals that don't find new families are still guaranteed a safe and happy place to live forever.

Best Friends works with groups all **a·round** the country to make the lives of animals better. They educate people about the importance of spaying and neutering pets. They also have the best interests of animals in mind when a crisis **oc·curs**. There's no doubt that the furry and feathered **crea·tures** of the world are lucky to have the folks at Best Friends looking out for them.

On the line, write the sound **y** makes in each bold word (long **i**, short **i**, **y**, or long **e**). Circle the word beside it that contains the same sound.

1. **typical**	____________	graciously	rhythm	nylon
2. **deny**	____________	policy	gypsy	magnify
3. **canyon**	____________	colony	yowl	mystery
4. **terribly**	____________	stingy	Egypt	gymnast
5. **crypt**	____________	occupy	yodel	physics

NAME ______________________________

Review Schwa, the Sounds of y, and r-controlled Vowels

Read the paragraphs below. Write each bold word beside the heading that contains the same **r**-controlled vowel sound.

Poetry can take many **forms**. It can be serious or humorous. Sometimes it rhymes, and sometimes there is a **particular** rhythm or beat. Because most poems are relatively **short**, words must be chosen **carefully**. Meaning is important because a poem often conveys a feeling or an experience. But the sound of the language is equally **important**. Words in a poem should fit **together** like puzzle pieces.

People who have made a **career** of writing poetry often give **similar sorts** of advice to young poets. They say that **brainstorming** is a good place to **start**. Instead of actively thinking of topics for a poem, **first** let your mind **wander**. Allow the thoughts to **swirl** around in your head. What moves you or makes you laugh? Where do you find beauty? What makes you feel **concerned** or lonely? When do you feel so happy your heart could **burst**?

Reading the work of other poets and becoming **familiar** with the language of poetry can help you become more comfortable using it and **sharing** it. Remember, there are as many different styles of poetry as there are poets. Check out the poetry of authors like William **Shakespeare**, Naomi Shihab Nye, Robert Frost, Shel **Silverstein**, and **Karla** Kuskin. Each of these poets has a unique voice, just as you do. What kind of poetry speaks to you?

carpet: ______________ ______________ ______________

______________ ______________

turning: ______________ ______________ ______________

______________ ______________ ______________

____

orchid: ______________ ______________ ______________

______________ ______________

fairly: ______________ ______________

clear: ______________ ______________

REVIEW: CHAPTER 1 LESSONS 14–17

NAME ____________________

Lesson 2.1 Base Words and Endings

A **base word** is a word without endings added to it.

- Double the consonant before adding **ed** or **ing** to a base word that has a short vowel sound and ends in a consonant.(snap, snap**ped**, snap**ping**)
- If a base word ends with **e**, drop the **e** before adding **ed** or **ing**. (excite, excit**ed**, excit**ing**)
- If a base word ends with **y**, change the **y** to **i** before adding **ed**. Do not change the **y** before adding **ing**. (occupy, occup**ied**, occup**ying**)

Fill in the blanks in the chart below.

Base Word	Add **ed**	Add **ing**
____________	____________	cherishing
struggle	____________	____________
____________	formatted	____________
scribble	____________	____________
enforce	____________	____________
____________	identified	____________
____________	untied	____________

On the line, write the base word for each word in bold.

1. The chef's hands were covered in food after she finished **demonstrating** ____________ to the class how to properly mix the ingredients.
2. Max **accompanied** ____________ Basir to his audition on Monday.
3. A road crew is **creating** ____________ a huge, muddy mess on our block while they repair the street.

Phonics Connection

Circle the words in the chart in which **y** makes the long **i** sound.

NAME ______________________________

Lesson 2.1 Base Words and Endings

Adding the endings **-s** or **-es** to base words forms new words.
- Adding **s** to the end of some verbs changes their form.
  Oliver and Lindsay cheer. Lindsay cheer**s**.
- If a verb ends with **y**, change the **y** to **i** and add **es**.
  The mice scurry. The mouse scurr**ies**.
- If a verb ends with **s**, **sh**, **ch**, **x**, or **z**, add **es**.
  The students rush. The student rush**es**.

Circle the words in parentheses that correctly complete the sentences below.

CFL (mean, means, meanes) *compact fluorescent lamp*. These special bulbs (fit, fits, fites) into the normal sockets of lamps and light fixtures. A CFL bulb (produce, produces) the same light as a regular bulb, but it (use, uses) a lot less energy. In fact, if you (switch, switchs, switches) to using CFL bulbs, you'll (save, saves) four times as much energy. CFL bulbs also (burn, burns, burnes) ten times as long, so you (purchase, purchases) them less often.

Ken Luna (teach, teachs, teaches) science to eighth graders in North Babylon, New York. He (wish, wishs, wishes) everyone would trade in their old-fashioned bulbs for CFLs. Mr. Luna (encourage, encourages) all of his students to use at least one CFL at home. To show them how dedicated he is to this plan, Mr. Luna (pass, passes) out a free bulb to each member of his class.

In his hometown of North Babylon, Mr. Luna's plan grew so popular that a hardware store donated 5,500 bulbs, one for each student in the city. This simple change (mean, means, meanes) that North Babylon residents will (save, saves) half a million dollars in energy costs each year!

If every household in the U.S. would (exchange, exchanges) just five regular light bulbs for CFL bulbs, the reduction in energy use and pollution would be like removing eight *million* cars from the nation's roads for one year!

NAME ______________________________

Lesson 2.2 Comparative Endings

The comparative endings -**er** and -**est** change the meanings of base words.

- Add **er** to mean *more* when comparing two things. Add **est** to mean *most* when comparing three or more things.
  deep**er** = more deep   deep**est** = most deep
- For words that end in **e**, drop the **e** and add **er** or **est**. For words that end in a consonant plus **y**, change the **y** to **i** before adding **er** or **est**.
  close, clos**er**, clos**est**   early, earl**ier**, earl**iest**
- For words that have a short vowel sound and end in a consonant, double the consonant before adding **er** or **est**.
  thin, thin**ner**, thin**nest**

Fill in the blanks below with the correct form of the comparative word.

Base Word	Add **er**	Add **est**
shiny	________	________
________	rarer	________
________	________	reddest
angry	________	________
________	________	lightest
________	________	loveliest
free	________	________
________	shallower	________
slim	________	________
strange	________	________
________	________	roughest
________	sleepier	________

NAME ______________________________

Lesson 2.2 Comparative Endings

Some comparisons are made by adding the word *more* or *most* in front of the adjective instead of adding an ending.

pleasant, **more** pleasant   valuable, **most** valuable

Read the paragraphs below. On the line, write the correct comparative form of the word in parentheses.

As the Fourth of July approaches each summer, Dante becomes the (excited) ______________ person in his family. Independence Day is the day Dante was born, and he loves the combined celebration. The Carroses' always pack their wagon with an old quilt and a picnic to take to the park. The wheels of the old red wagon grow (squeaky) ______________ every year, but no one seems to care.

The year Dante turned nine was the (frustrating) ______________ birthday of his life. One of the wheels snapped off the wagon, pasta salad scattered all over the sidewalk, and Dante's little sister spilled juice on the quilt. Luckily, the rest of Dante's birthday celebrations have gone a bit (smoothly) ______________.

Every year, the Carros family gets into a good-natured argument as they pull the wagon eight blocks to Freedom Park. Mr. Carros and Dante argue that the (interesting) ______________ view of the fireworks is from Dobbin Hill. Mrs. Carros tries to convince the family to leave (early) ______________ than usual so that they can find seats for the show in the gazebo. That's where the (popular) ______________ seats are, but Grandma Louise thinks it's (safe) ______________ to watch fireworks from a distance. After all the debate, the Carroses end up spreading their quilt on the grassy slope of a hill, just like they do every year.

NAME ______________________________

Review Base Words and Endings

Read the paragraphs below. Add **ed** or **ing** to each word in parentheses, and write the new word on the line. The form of the word you choose should make sense in the sentence.

When you hear the words *star-spangled banner*, the song by Francis Scott Key probably begins (play) __________________ in your mind. However, most people know little about the flag that (inspire) __________________ the famous song.

In 1813, Major George Armistead took over command of Fort McHenry in Baltimore, Maryland. He (hire) __________________ a woman (name) __________________ Mary Pickersgill to sew two flags. The larger of the flags (measure) __________________ 30 by 42 feet when it was (complete) __________________. Although Mary had some help from her daughter, nieces, and a servant, (sew) __________________ the flag was literally an enormous job. (The open flag would cover about half of a tennis court!) Even so, the talented seamstress (finish) __________________ the job in about two months. The Star Spangled Banner had 15 stars and 15 stripes and cost $405.90.

The smaller storm flag had been (fly) __________________ on the evening of September 13, 1814, as the British (try) __________________ to take Fort McHenry. The American soldiers fought hard, bravely (defend) __________________ the city of Baltimore, and the British troops finally withdrew. In the morning, the large Star Spangled Banner replaced the storm flag and could be seen for miles. It (wave) __________________ proudly and (announce) __________________ the American victory.

NAME ____________________

Review Base Words and Endings

Read each 6th-grade candidate's campaign slogans. Underline the word or words from the set in parentheses that correctly complete the sentences.

Danny Calbert for President 2008!

- Your choice couldn't be (easier, easiest). Vote for Calbert for class president, and you'll be sure you did the right thing.
- Want a class president who knows how to make you laugh? Vote for Danny Calbert: he's the (funnyest, funniest) candidate in '08!
- Danny promises to bring the (later, latest) technology to our classrooms as president. Don't get left behind—vote for Danny!

Austin Young: Your Voice in Student Politics

- Are you looking for a (kindest, kinder), (gentler, gentleer) student government? Austin is the (most compassionate, compassionatest) candidate for president, but he's also the (tougher, toughest).
- Austin Young: Straight A's two years in a row. Don't you want the (smartest, most smart) candidate working for you?
- Austin has the (originalest, most original) ideas for 2008. A vote for Austin is a vote for a (brightest, brighter) future.

Cristina Wang—Leadership and Experience

- Cristina may be (youngest, younger) than the competition, but no one else has her experience and know-how in student government.
- Vote Cristina, your (most trustworthy, trustworthiest) choice for president, and let your voice be heard.
- Want (healthiest, healthier) choices in the cafeteria, (more interesting, intrestinger) field trips, and a (biger, bigger) gym? Elect Cristina Wang!

Next to each word below, write its base word.

dripping ____________	relaxes ____________	polishes ____________
occupying ____________	dragged ____________	empties ____________

NAME ____________________

Lesson 2.3 Plurals

Most plural words are formed by adding **s** to the end of a word.
workbook, workbook**s** elevator, elevator**s**

- If a noun ends in **sh**, **ch**, **s**, or **x**, add **es**. dress, dress**es**
- If a noun ends with a consonant and **y**, drop the **y** and add **ies**. family, famil**ies**
- Form the plural of most words that end in **f** by just adding **s**. cliff, cliff**s** For some words that end in **f** or **fe**, change the **f** or **fe** to **v** and add **es**. knife, kni**ves**

On the lines below, write the correct plural of each word in parentheses.

If you live in the Southeast, you may have noticed an interesting plant covering ________________ (tree) and ________________ (bush), ________________ (house), and telephone ________________ (pole). In ________________ (story) passed down through the generations, kudzu is known as the *mile-a-minute vine*, the *foot-a-night vine*, and the *vine that ate the South*. Originally, it grew only in the southern parts of Asian ________________ (country), like China and Japan. In 1876, it was brought to America as an ornamental plant. People liked the dark green ________________ (leaf) and fragrant ________________ (bloom).

During the Depression, ________________ (mass) of kudzu ________________ (vine) were planted to help prevent soil erosion. The problem was that the ________________ (condition) were too perfect in the South. The vines covered the ________________ (branch) of trees, ________________ (bridge), buildings, ________________ (roof)—anything that didn't move. When the plants were brought to the U.S., none of their natural ________________ (enemy) came along. During the summer, kudzu can grow as much as a foot a day! It cuts short the ________________ (life) of whatever plants or trees it covers. It's no surprise that in 1953, the Department of Agriculture stopped recommending its use.

NAME ____________________

Lesson 2.3 Plurals

- Form the plural of a word that ends with a vowel plus **o** by adding **s**.
  video, video**s** zoo, zoo**s**
- Form the plural of a word that ends with a consonant and **o** by adding **es**.
  cargo, cargo**es** halo, halo**es**
- Some words, such as *photo*, *piano*, and *rhino*, do not follow this pattern. Just add **s** to make their plurals. Use a dictionary to check plural spellings.

Choose the word from the box that matches each clue below and write it on the line. Then, find the plural form of the word in the word search puzzle.

pistachio	solo	flamingo	tomato	burrito	pueblo	kangaroo

1. a juicy red fruit that is usually used as a vegetable ____________
2. an Australian animal that carries its young in a pouch ____________
3. a light green edible nut ____________
4. a tortilla stuffed with meat, rice, beans, and cheese ____________
5. a bright pink tropical bird that has long, skinny legs ____________
6. to do something alone ____________
7. a Native American village or community of the Southwest ____________

p	r	m	a	a	h	u	r	u	p	n	f	s	g
n	i	b	d	p	l	b	u	r	r	i	t	o	s
g	s	s	e	o	g	n	i	m	a	l	f	w	q
l	s	p	t	v	f	u	i	e	m	a	x	z	p
s	o	o	r	a	g	n	a	k	c	x	p	u	r
b	l	t	y	w	c	c	d	a	j	h	e	i	r
e	o	k	j	c	b	h	e	t	w	b	g	k	n
l	s	l	y	f	o	d	i	t	l	u	b	a	o
d	j	r	e	n	w	p	v	o	z	h	y	e	e
t	o	m	a	t	o	e	s	g	s	j	m	u	q

NAME ______________________________

Lesson 2.4 Irregular Plurals

Some words have **irregular plural forms**.

child, children   foot, feet   die, dice   goose, geese
ox, oxen   woman, women   man, men   mouse, mice
tooth, teeth   parenthesis, parentheses   oasis, oases

The singular and plural forms of the following words are the same: *deer*, *fish*, *moose*, *sheep*, *trout*, *salmon*, *wheat*, *series*, *traffic*, and *species*.

Read the sentences below. Underline the word from the pair in parentheses that correctly completes each sentence.

1. Seven (children, child) in Mohammed's class live in his neighborhood.
2. How many (trouts, trout) did you catch last weekend?
3. The tallest player for the Valley Ridge Pistons is nearly six (feet, foots) tall, and she is only 13 years old.
4. The exhausted traveler thought he saw an (oasis, oases) in the desert, but it turned out to be only an illusion.
5. Do you know how many (species, specieses) of frogs the researchers discovered in the rain forest?
6. After wearing braces for three years, Kiara's (teeths, teeth) are nearly perfect.
7. A small gray (mice, mouse) with velvety fur and pink ears scurried across the kitchen floor.
8. The three (deer, deers) stood motionless in the woods, waiting for the intruder to pass.
9. The naturalist knew how to set the (geese's, goose's) broken wing so that it would heal properly.

NAME ______________________

Lesson 2.4 Irregular Plurals

Ms. Mihocik's class is having a competition to see who can write the most creative or intriguing first line to a story. Read the students' entries below. Then, write a new first line using the plural form of each bold word.

1. By the time the snow reached the windows of Anna's cabin, she knew she had no choice—she'd have to remove the infected **tooth** herself.

   ____

2. As Mr. Wales drove home from work, he noticed that his car was the only car headed east, and that the rest of the **traffic** sped quickly away from the city.

   ____

3. The young **woman** stared at the mirror in disbelief, unable to recognize a single feature of her face.

   ____

4. Eduardo yanked as hard as he could on the thin, taut line and began reeling in what he assumed was just a very large **fish**.

   ____

5. The anxious fans who filled the stadium waited in silence to see if the star forward would be able to play on her injured **foot**.

   ____

6. Kate could see clouds of steam rising from the **moose's** nostrils as she carefully backed away from the animal's glinting eyes and bony antlers.

   ____

Phonics Connection

1. On the lines, write the bold words from above that contain a digraph.

   ______________________ ______________________

2. Which two bold words contain the /ü/ sound? ______________________

   ______________________ Which word contains the /u̇/ sound? ______________________

NAME ______________________________

Lesson 2.5 Possessives

Form a **possessive**, or word that shows ownership, by adding an apostrophe (') and an **s** to the end of a word. Words that end in **s** are treated the same way.

Jacob**'s** bedroom   Jess**'s** team

To form a **plural possessive**, add an apostrophe to the end of a plural word.

the cars' headlights   the babies' pacifiers

If a plural word does not end in **s**, add an apostrophe plus **s**.

the sheep**'s** wool   the women**'s** goal

Read the paragraphs below. If the bold word is plural, write **PL** on the line. If it is singular possessive, write **SP**. If it is plural possessive, write **PP**.

Most people are familiar with the Olympic Games, but few know much about the Paralympic Games. They are intended for people with physical **disabilities** ______, and the **competitors'** ______ determination and skills are amazing to witness.

The first competitions were **London's** ______ Stoke Mandeville Games, held in 1948 for veterans of World War II. As a doctor, Ludwig **Guttmann's** ______ purpose in founding the event was to give people with spinal cord injuries a chance to develop physically and increase their self-confidence. Other **countries** ______ joined the competition during the next few years, and in 1960, the first Paralympics were held in Rome. Today, a host **city's** ______ bid for the Olympic Games includes the Paralympics, which use the same **facilities** ______ and take place three weeks after the close of the Olympics.

The **sports** ______ include swimming, sailing, basketball, fencing, wheelchair rugby, volleyball, wheelchair tennis, judo, alpine skiing, and sledge hockey, among many others. The **sports'** ______ rules may be slightly modified to fit a particular disability, but generally, there are not a great number of differences.

NAME ______________________

Lesson 2.5 Possessives

Read the sentences below. On the line, write the possessive form of each word in parentheses.

1. March is National (Women) ________________ History Month.
2. The (event) ________________ goal is to bring awareness to women's issues and celebrate the achievements of women in many different fields.
3. Maya (Angelou) ________________ famous book *I Know Why the Caged Bird Sings* was published in 1970.
4. Rachel Carson, a biologist and nature writer, wrote a book that brought the (world) ________________ attention to the dangers of a chemical called *DDT*.
5. Maya Lin, a sculptor and architect, may be best known for submitting the winning design for the Vietnam (Veterans) ________________ Memorial in Washington, D.C.
6. Wilma Mankiller, the Cherokee (Nation) ________________ Chief from 1985 to 1995, was the first woman to lead a large Native American tribe.
7. Of all the space (shuttles) ________________ commanders, only one has been a woman: Eileen Collins.

Rewrite each phrase below as a possessive.

1. the beat of the drums ________________
2. the lyrics of the song ________________
3. the solo of the guitarist ________________
4. the energy of the musicians ________________
5. the melody of the keyboard ________________

NAME ____________________

Review Plurals, Irregular Plurals, and Possessives

Fill in the blanks to complete the chart below.

Singular	Plural	Singular Possessive	Plural Possessive
colony	______	______	______
______	______	waltz's	______
coach	______	______	______
______	______	banjo's	______
city	______	______	______
______	______	______	portfolios'
______	physicians	______	______
______	mice	______	______
______	______	mosquito's	______

Read the sentences below. Underline the word from the pair in parentheses that correctly completes each sentence.

1. Andy enjoys reading nonfiction and usually chooses (biographies, biographys) or true-adventure (storyes, stories).
2. Tanner prefers (mysterys, mysteries) and crime (novels, noveles).
3. Dwarves, (elfs, elves), and (ogres, ogres') are not uncommon characters in the (folktales, folktaleses) and (legends, legendes) that Shelby reads.
4. Natalie has a large collection of Japanese (comices, comics) that she orders from online specialty stores.
5. All three sixth-grade (class's, classes) at Washington Heights Middle School are reading J. R. R. Tolkien's book *The Hobbit*.
6. Sydney and Evan love looking through their mom's (cookbooks, cookbookes) and making interesting (recipies, recipes), like Cheesy Chicken (Burritoes, Burritos) or Upside-Down Cake with (Mangoes, Mango's).

NAME ______________________

Review Plurals, Irregular Plurals, and Possessives

The possessives have been written incorrectly in the announcements below. On each line, rewrite the correct form of the possessive and its object.

1. Join Harris Books' Literate Ladys' Reading Club! ______________________
2. Learn drawing, painting, or ceramics at the Watman Recreation Center. Call 555-3423 for all the class's schedules. ______________________
3. On 3/23/07, my mothers purse was left behind at Billy's BBQ Palace. Please call with any information: 555-9895. Reward offered! ______________________
4. For sale: 30 assorted childs toys—$15 or best offer. ______________________
5. Volunteers needed! Help clean Johnson Park this Sunday. Each persons' participation will be rewarded with a picnic lunch! ______________________
6. A benefit auction will be held for Jake Masters. Help raise funds to help pay for Jakes internship in the Brazilian rain forest. ______________________
7. New, advanced fishing-lure technology! Trouts' mouths just can't wait to bite onto this bait! Call 1-800-555-3938 for more details! ______________________

REVIEW: CHAPTER 2 LESSONS 3–5

Phonics Connection

1. On the lines, write the two words in the exercise above in which the digraph **ch** is pronounced /k/. ______________ ______________
2. On the lines, write the two words that contain a vowel pair that makes the sound you hear in ***raw***. ______________ ______________

NAME ______________________________

Lesson 2.6 Compound Words

A **compound word** is a combination of two shorter words.

hand + shake = handshake candle + stick = candlestick

Some words are called **open compounds**. In open compounds, there is a space between the two words, but they refer to a single thing.

home run high school

Use the pictures to help you fill in the blanks in the problems below.

1.  +  = ______________________

2.  +  = ______________________

3. bare +  = ______________________

4.  +  = ______________________

5.  + 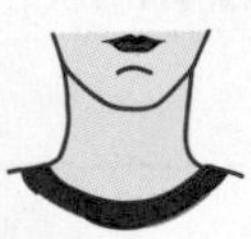 = ______________________

6. jelly +  = ______________________

Form a common compound word by drawing a line to match each word in column 1 to a word in column 2. Write the compound word on the line.

1. water	pool	______________
2. loud	engine	______________
3. whirl	weed	______________
4. fire	melon	______________
5. sea	speaker	______________

NAME ______________________

Lesson 2.6 Compound Words

Read the letter below. Circle the 12 compound words, and draw a slash (/) between the two parts of each compound. You do not need to mark the same word more than once.

Dear Friends and Neighbors,

We, the kids of Fulton-Kings neighborhood, are writing to you with a very important message. If you have read the local newspaper recently, you are probably aware of the discussion surrounding the empty lot at the corner of Benson Avenue and 8th Street. The city intends to turn the lot into a dump for non-hazardous materials.

As you know, many Fulton-Kings residents live in apartments or homes with small backyards. Wouldn't you rather your children spent their afternoons and weekends outdoors instead of being cooped up inside?

This is why we would like to propose that a park be built in place of the dump. Several parents have volunteered to help build a playground. Stebbins Nursery is willing to donate plants for landscaping, as well as a small greenhouse for the community garden. We'd also like to have a basketball court, a large sandbox, and a pond.

We are asking all the residents of Fulton-Kings to take the time to sign our petition. You can also e-mail the mayor's office (vestevez@city.gov) or the city commissioner (tazewell@city.gov) and let your opinions about this project be heard. Without your help, the newest addition to our neighborhood will be a dump. Isn't it worthwhile to help us make a positive change?

Sincerely,

Darius, Alex, Breanna, Mackenzie, Nasira, Kayla, Robert, Tasha, Dinh, Vanessa, Sammy

NAME ______________________________

Lesson 2.7 Contractions

- A **contraction** is an abbreviated way of writing two words. An apostrophe (') takes the place of the missing letters in a contraction.
  I've = I have   doesn't = does not   you'll = you will
- The words *will* and *not* form the contraction *won't.*

Underline the correct contraction in each set of parentheses below.

(There're, The're) probably a number of foods you (are'nt, aren't) too crazy about eating. (I'd, I'ld) guess that certain vegetables are at the top of your list, but you probably (have'nt, haven't) ever needed to politely refuse a plate full of insects. People around the world eat all kinds of things (I'am, I'm) guessing (you'd, you'ld) never imagine making a meal from.

For instance, in Colombia, (do'nt, don't) be surprised if you see people eating fried ants. (The're, They're) served in paper cones and eaten as a snack similar to popcorn. A Colombian (won't, wo'nt) hesitate to eat a guinea pig, either. (It's, Its') a common source of meat in South America.

In New Zealand, (they've, th'ave) been eating grubs for centuries. Hu Hu grubs (aren't, are'nt) just for the native Maori people, though. Many New Zealanders of European descent, and plenty of tourists, like them, too. (They'ill, They'll) tell you that the grubs taste like peanut butter.

Now, (let's, lets's) head north to Japan and Korea, where some restaurants serve sea slugs as a delicacy. You (might've, might'ave) thought that sea slugs could be tasty if the cook has drizzled a flavorful sauce over them, but (heres, here's) the problem: sea slugs are eaten alive!

One of France's most famous dishes is escargot cooked in a garlicky butter sauce. Maybe (your, you're) thinking that sounds tasty, but you (shouldn't, should'nt) decide until I translate the dish's name into English. *Escargot* is the French word for *snails.* (What're, What'er) you thinking now?

NAME ______________________

Lesson 2.7 Contractions

Each of the following sentences contains one incorrect contraction. Circle the contraction and rewrite it correctly on the line.

1. I've been waiting for years to try something I have'nt done before: parachuting. ______________
2. Next week, Im going skydiving with someone who's jumped more than a hundred times. ______________
3. My instructors shown me everything I should and shouldn't do while falling through the air. ______________
4. We've even jumped off a tall platform so that the impact when I land wo'nt be a surprise. ______________
5. I'm confident about the landing; thats not what's bothering me. ______________
6. I keep dreaming that theres a strong wind that carries me far away from where I should've landed. ______________
7. For the last two nights, I have'nt slept well. ______________
8. I mustn't stay up too late the night before because were taking off early in the morning. ______________
9. My instructor assured me today that we'll do just fine, and if the winds too strong, we wouldn't be jumping anyway. ______________

Phonics Connection

1. Find four words from the exercise above that contain the same long **a** vowel pair and write them on the lines.

______________ ______________

______________ ______________

2. Find two words in which the /sh/ sound is not spelled **sh** and write them on the lines.

______________ ______________

NAME ______________________________

Review Compound Words and Contractions

Read the words in both boxes below. On the lines that follow, combine the words to make as many compound words as possible.

Box A (first half of compound)
fire any home under

Box B (second half of compound)
body place ground fly grown
one room town sick wood
thing fighter where water wear
bag more made cover works

_______________ _______________ _______________ _______________

_______________ _______________ _______________ _______________

_______________ _______________ _______________ _______________

_______________ _______________ _______________ _______________

_______________ _______________

Unscramble the bold letters and write the compound word that matches each clue below. Draw a slash (/) to separate the two words in each compound.

1. bread made with ground corn **adcrberno** _______________
2. a skate used for moving around on ice **eic kstea** _______________
3. a cup used for drinking tea **ctaepu** _______________
4. a print made by a foot **fnopirott** _______________
5. to ride on the back of a horse **sebahocrk** _______________
6. light from a candle **elictdlghan** _______________
7. a hive in which bees live **vehiebe** _______________
8. a bear that lives in polar regions **olapr brae** _______________
9. a hole in which a button fits **hobtlonute** _______________

REVIEW: CHAPTER 2 LESSONS 6–7

NAME ______________________________

Review Compound Words and Contractions

Circle the contractions in the sentences below. Write the two words that make up each contraction on the lines that follow the sentence.

1. If you're interested in music, you should visit the Rock and Roll Hall of Fame in Cleveland, Ohio.

   ______________ ______________

2. However, if you are expecting to see relatively new artists, you'll probably be disappointed.

   ______________ ______________

3. A musician can't be inducted until 25 years after his or her first record is released.

   ______________ ______________

4. It's probably the best place in the country to learn about the history of rock music and the performers who made it famous.

   ______________ ______________

5. Cleveland wasn't the only city that wanted the Hall of Fame, but 600,000 residents signed petitions and won the honor for their hometown.

   ______________ ______________

6. All the inductees aren't American and British, but some people feel that rockers from other countries haven't been given enough attention.

   ______________ ______________ ______________ ______________

7. You shouldn't plan to visit the museum if you don't have plenty of time to spend looking at the impressive collections.

   ______________ ______________ ______________ ______________

8. There're thousands of rare artifacts from artists like the Beatles, Elvis Presley, the Rolling Stones, U2, and Michael Jackson.

   ______________ ______________

NAME ____________________

Lesson 2.8 Prefixes

> Adding a **prefix** to the beginning of a base word can change its meaning.
> - The prefixes **in-**, **im-**, **ir-**, and **il-** all mean *not*.
>
> | | |
> |---|---|
> | **im**pure = not pure | **in**convenient = not convenient |
> | **il**legal = not legal | **ir**responsible = not responsible |

Read the paragraphs below. Circle the 13 words that contain the prefixes **in-**, **im-**, **ir-**, or **il-**.

Normally, my brother, Will, and I are inseparable. We have a lot of fun together and our disagreements are infrequent. Last weekend, though, we had a fight our parents described as immature and irrational.

After breakfast that morning, Will asked if I would help him with a project. Working with my older brother is always an irresistible treat, so I quickly agreed. Will explained that we were going to move a pile of stones from the front of the house to the garden in the backyard. By the time I got the wheelbarrow, my brother stood impatiently waiting to get started. We quickly loaded the cart with small stones, which we took turns wheeling to the garden. I thought it was inefficient, because one of us just stood there half the time.

The stones became bigger as we reached the bottom of the pile. The last stone was practically immovable. My brother insisted that we lift it into the wheelbarrow, but I thought that was illogical. I suggested that the stone would be easier to roll around the house. Will didn't seem to like the fact that his little brother had come up with a better idea. He claimed that my inexperience in landscape work made me incapable of knowing how to handle the rock.

Our comments became increasingly impolite and increasingly loud. That was when our parents came outside to see what was happening. To Will's credit, he did apologize a few days later and admitted that he was incorrect about the best way to move the stone. Yet another reason I admire my brother!

NAME ____________________

Lesson 2.8 Prefixes

- The prefixes **en**- and **em**- mean *in, into, make,* or *cause to.*
  enlarge = make large

Read each pair of sentences below. Complete them with a pair of words from the box. The words you choose should fit the context of the sentences.

envisioned, ensured	enrolled, employed	enlisted, enriched	engulf, encouraged

1. The fire chief waited for the flames to __________________ the building before allowing the firefighters-in-training to put it out.

2. The veteran firefighters stood at the sidelines and __________________ the men and women who faced the blaze.

---

3. On August 23, Mr. Hopple __________________ his three-year-old triplets at Sunnyside Preschool.

4. Mr. Hopple had been __________________ by the school as a teacher for six years, but recently he decided to teach at the elementary school.

---

5. Margaret Fernandez __________________ in the army when she graduated from college.

6. Looking back on her years in the military, Margaret felt that the experience had

   __________________ her life.

---

7. Miles spent three weekends in a row trying to create the project he had

   __________________ as his entry for the science fair.

8. Once he __________________ that everything worked exactly as planned, Miles helped his dad load the bulky machine into the minivan.

NAME ____________________

Lesson 2.8 Prefixes

- The prefix **co**- means *together*. **co**captain = to be captains together
- The prefix **mid**- means *middle*. **mid**day = middle of the day
- The prefix **re**- means *again*. **re**unite = unite again

Read each clue below. Underline the word in parentheses that matches the clue. On the line, write the base word.

1. to host something together (cohost, rehost) ____________
2. the middle of a stream (costream, midstream) ____________
3. to produce again (reproduce, coproduce) ____________
4. to write again (cowrite, rewrite) ____________

Circle the word with a prefix in each sentence below. On the line, write the definition of the word.

1. Anna's parents cofounded the Beckwith Little Theater 12 years ago.

   ____

2. They had both loved performing as children and were excited to rediscover their hobby with Anna and her brother. ____________________

3. In June, they began auditions for the lead in the midsummer production.

   ____

4. It was cowritten by two teachers from Anna's school. ____________________

   ____

5. They retold a famous Shakespeare play but set it in modern times.

   ____

6. After watching the rehearsal, the Beckwiths felt reassured that the play would be a great success. ____________________

NAME ______________________

Lesson 2.8 Prefixes

- The prefix **inter**- means *between* or *among*. **inter**state = between states
- The prefix **semi**- means *partly* or *half*. **semi**sweet = partly sweet
- The prefix **non**- means *not*. **non**productive = not productive

Read the words and the clues below. Circle the prefixes in the words in the second column. On the line, write the letter of the word that matches each clue.

1. ______	partly conscious	**a.** semisolid
2. ______	connect among one another	**b.** nonacademic
3. ______	not factual	**c.** semicircle
4. ______	half solid	**d.** nonfiction
5. ______	between nations	**e.** interconnect
6. ______	not academic	**f.** intercoastal
7. ______	partly dry	**g.** intercollegiate
8. ______	not fiction	**h.** semiconscious
9. ______	between coasts	**i.** nonspecific
10. ______	half a circle	**j.** international
11. ______	not specific	**k.** semidry
12. ______	between colleges	**l.** nonfactual

Phonics Connection

Use the words in column 2 to answer the questions that follow.

1. On the lines, write the words that contain the soft **c** and soft **g** sounds.

______________________ ______________________ ______________________

2. Which two words contain both the soft and hard sounds of **c**?

______________________ ______________________

NAME ______________________

Lesson 2.8 Prefixes

• The prefix **uni**- means *one.*	**uni**color = one color
• The prefix **bi**- means *two.*	**bi**monthly = happening every two months
• The prefix **tri**- means *three.*	**tri**angle = having three angles
• The prefix **multi**- means *many.*	**multi**level = having many levels

Read the questions and the choices that follow. Underline the word that matches each description.

1. What is a competition in which athletes compete in three sports?

   triathlon   multilevel   biathlon

2. What are eyeglasses that contain two different types of lenses called?

   trifocals   bifocals   multifocals

3. What is the name for a person who speaks many languages?

   trilingual   bilingual   multilingual

4. What is something that is a single color called?

   multicolor   tricolor   unicolor

5. What is the name for a celebration that marks 200 years?

   bicentennial   tricentennial   multicentennial

6. What is the name for a mythical creature that has a single horn on its head?

   biped   unicorn   tripod

7. What is an event that deals with people from many cultures called?

   multicultural   unicultural   bicultural

8. What is the name for a series of three books?

   biology   multipack   trilogy

9. What is something that can be used for many different purposes called?

   multipurpose   bipurpose   tripurpose

NAME ______________________

Lesson 2.8 Prefixes

- The prefix **dis**- means *not* or *opposite of.* **dis**honest = not honest
- The prefix **mis**- means *wrongly* or *badly.* **mis**read = read wrongly

Replace each set of bold words below with a word using **mis** or **dis**.

Last week, my friend Thomas and I had a bit of a **bad understanding** ______________ with our teacher, Mrs. Younger. Our class had gone to a park to gather leaves and twigs to make a nature collage. Mrs. Younger had asked that everyone not **badly treat** ______________ the privilege of a special day away from class by **not obeying** ______________ her rules.

Thomas and I decided to check out a path that ran into the woods. Thomas assured me he knew the perfect place to find cool leaves. The problem was that Thomas **badly judged** ______________ how well he knew the park. He **wrongly led** ______________ us onto a path he didn't recognize, and we were lost.

For an hour we hiked up and down a bunch of different paths. We tried not to get **not encouraged** ______________, but we knew Mrs. Younger was going to be mad because we had **not appeared** ______________ into the woods.

Finally, we found a way out. Mrs. Younger was **not pleased** ______________ with us, to say the least.

She was frustrated by our **bad behavior** ______________, but mostly she was worried that something had happened. We promised to use better judgment next time, and Mrs. Younger said she had no doubt we would. What a day!

NAME ____________________

Lesson 2.9 Suffixes

Adding a **suffix** to the end of a base word can change its meaning. Sometimes the spelling of a base word must change before an ending is added. For example, you may need to drop a final **e**, double a final consonant, or change a **y** to **i** before adding a suffix.

- The suffixes -**sion** and -**tion** mean the *act of*, *state of*, or *quality of*.
  confu**sion** = state of being confused   opera**tion** = the act of operating

Read the paragraphs below. Circle the 15 words that contain the suffixes -**sion** and -**tion**. Do not mark the same word more than once.

Animation is the illusion created by making unmoving objects in different positions appear to move. It is a sort of deception of the human eye. The images pass so quickly that your brain connects each frame in one continuous movement. Animators usually create 24 frames per each second of film. If you do some calculations, you'll see how much time, energy, and attention go into the production of a single television cartoon or feature film.

In the past, animation was done completely by hand. In addition to being able to create interesting illustrations, an animator needed to work with precision, concentration, and great patience. Cel animation was used for the first time in the early 1900s, and it sped things up a bit. Using transparent overlays saved the animators time because they did not need to re-create the entire background for every frame.

Nothing changed the world of animation more, however, than the invention of the computer. Not all modern animation is created digitally, but the obvious attraction of using a computer is how much time can be saved. Computer animation can also be incredibly realistic. Most computer animated figures are three-dimensional, a quality that brings the characters to life in a way that almost nothing else can.

NAME ______________________

Lesson 2.9 Suffixes

- The suffixes -**er** and -**or** can mean *a person who*.
  garden**er** = a person who gardens   direct**or** = a person who directs
- The suffix -**ist** means *one who makes or practices*.
  pian**ist** = someone who plays the piano

Read each phrase below. On the line that follows, write a sentence using a word that replaces the phrase and contains the suffix -**er**, -**or**, or -**ist**.

Ex.: a person who speaks
The Speaker of the House is a powerful position in the U.S. House of Representatives.

1. a person who paints

____

2. a person who invents

____

3. one who creates novels

____

4. a person who governs

____

5. one who studies biology

____

6. a person who collects

____

7. a person who boxes

____

8. a person who conducts

____

NAME ______________________

Lesson 2.9 Suffixes

- The suffixes -**ness** and -**ship** mean *state of being* or *condition of.*
  rough**ness** = state of being rough   partner**ship** = state of being a partner
- The suffixes -**ance** and -**ence** mean *state of being* or *the act of.*
  guid**ance** = the act of guiding   exist**ence** = the state of existing

Add a suffix to each base word below. Write the new word on the first line. On the second line, write the definition of the word. Then, circle each word in the word search puzzle. Words may be written forward, backward, or diagonally.

1. fair + ness = ______________ ______________________________

2. occur + ence = ______________ ______________________________

3. assist + ance = ______________ ______________________________

4. companion + ship = ______________ ______________________________

5. round + ness = ______________ ______________________________

6. fragrant + ance = ______________ ______________________________

7. innocent + ence = ______________ ______________________________

8. citizen + ship = ______________ ______________________________

o	p	i	h	s	n	o	i	n	a	p	m	o	c
e	c	i	t	i	z	e	n	s	h	i	p	l	s
s	e	c	n	e	c	o	n	n	i	d	f	o	s
s	y	b	u	n	s	s	w	p	h	a	j	x	e
e	m	t	f	r	a	g	r	a	n	c	e	c	n
n	o	r	m	a	r	q	j	c	b	i	u	f	d
r	r	y	i	b	v	e	d	g	w	q	i	z	n
i	l	l	p	e	b	n	n	s	h	r	v	a	u
a	s	s	i	s	t	a	n	c	e	m	e	r	o
f	p	t	b	d	u	a	q	r	e	n	x	o	r

NAME ____________________

Lesson 2.9 Suffixes

- The suffix -**ly** means *in a way.* quiet**ly** = in a quiet way
- The suffix -**y** means *being* or *having.* luck**y** = having luck
- The suffixes -**al** and -**ial** mean *like* or *having the characteristic of.*
  coast**al** = having the characteristics of the coast
  industr**ial** = having the characteristics of industry

Circle the 23 words below that end with the suffix -**ly**, -**y**, -**al**, or -**ial**.

On a steamy day in August, Julia O'Brien boarded a plane for Ireland. She had wanted for years to see her family's ancestral home. When she finally stood before the modest cottage, Julia felt herself becoming teary. It sat alone on a small, grassy hill, the windows winking brightly in the afternoon sun. It was just a traditional Irish cottage, but to Julia, there was something almost magical about seeing the house where generations of her ancestors had been born. The house's mossy walls and friendly face immediately made Julia feel like she had come home.

"It might smell a bit stuffy or musty when you first go inside," said a kindly voice behind Julia, "but I've tried to air it out at least once a week. It's essential when we have long spells of rainy weather."

Julia turned around abruptly to see a small woman with a halo of white hair, inky black eyes, and a cheerful grin.

"I'm Maggie Flanagan," the woman added helpfully. "I've lived next door to the O'Briens my whole life."

Julia smiled, glad to see a cheery face. "I was worried that my family's history would be lost if I didn't come along to claim it," she said thoughtfully.

Mrs. Flanagan nodded and gently took Julia's arm. "You'd have your grandma's approval if she were here. She was the family memory-keeper, just like you."

NAME ______________________________

Lesson 2.9 Suffixes

The suffixes -**ous** and -**ious** mean *having the quality of.*

disastr**ous** = having the quality of a disaster
superstit**ious** = having the quality of superstition

Read each base word below. Add the suffix -**ous** or -**ious** and write the new word on the first line. On the second line, write a sentence using the word you formed. Remember, you may need to alter the spelling of the base word .

1. adventure → ____________________

   ____

2. infect → ____________________

   ____

3. miracle → ____________________

   ____

4. caution → ____________________

   ____

5. ambition → ____________________

   ____

6. fury → ____________________

   ____

Phonics Connection

Use the words you formed in exercise 1 to answer the questions below.

1. In which words does **ti** make the /sh/ sound?

   ____________________ ____________________ ____________________

2. On the lines, write the three words that contain **r**-controlled vowels.

   ____________________ ____________________ ____________________

NAME ______________________________

Lesson 2.9 Suffixes

Some words have more than one suffix.

thirst**iness** (-y, -ness)	realis**tically** (-ic, -al, -ly)
motiva**tional** (-tion, -al)	hope**fully** (-ful, -ly)

Circle the word or words that contain more than one suffix in each sentence below. Make a slash (/) between the two suffixes.

1. Even though our field trip to the Wilson Zoological Gardens was for educational purposes, everyone still had a lot of fun.
2. A long line of people waited expectantly to get into the zoo that day, but our class entered effortlessly through a side door.
3. The zookeeper led us past a wide pond where dozens of birds gracefully glided through the water or waddled across the green carpet created by the ground's mossiness.
4. In the reptile house, the zookeeper unlatched a fastener that held the top on an aquarium, then cautiously pulled out a six-foot python.
5. While the zookeeper fed lunch to the snake—disgustingly made up of live mice—our teacher described the realistic way the snake would have caught its food in the wild.
6. In the bat house, bats flitted jerkily around the cage and strategically maneuvered through the air to reach dangling pieces of fruit.
7. As the zookeeper spoke in a conversational tone to two giant brown bears, she casually tossed chunks of meat into their exceptionally clean cage.
8. The spotlessness of the bears' cage surprised me, until I learned that each cage is regularly hosed out—twice a day.
9. Everyone in our group smiled and laughed at the companionship of the bears, as they playfully wrestled after eating lunch.

NAME ______________________________

Review Prefixes and Suffixes

Use the table to help you remember the meanings of the prefixes you learned.

in-, **im-**, **ir-**, **il-**, **non-**, **dis-** = not			**semi-** = half, partly
en-, **em-** = in, into, or make			**inter-** = between, among
mid- = middle			**co-** = together
re- = again			**mis-** = wrongly or badly
uni- = one	**bi-** = two	**tri-** = three	**multi-** = many

Read the clues below. Choose the word from the box that matches each clue. Write the answers in the numbered spaces in the crossword puzzle.

rearrange	inexpensive	dishonest	nonspecific	enlarge	
misjudge	interstate	coexist	semiprivate	triceratops	immature

Across

3. to exist together
7. between states
8. a horned dinosaur
9. not expensive
10. to make larger
11. to wrongly judge

Down

1. not specific
2. not mature
4. partly private
5. arrange again
6. not honest

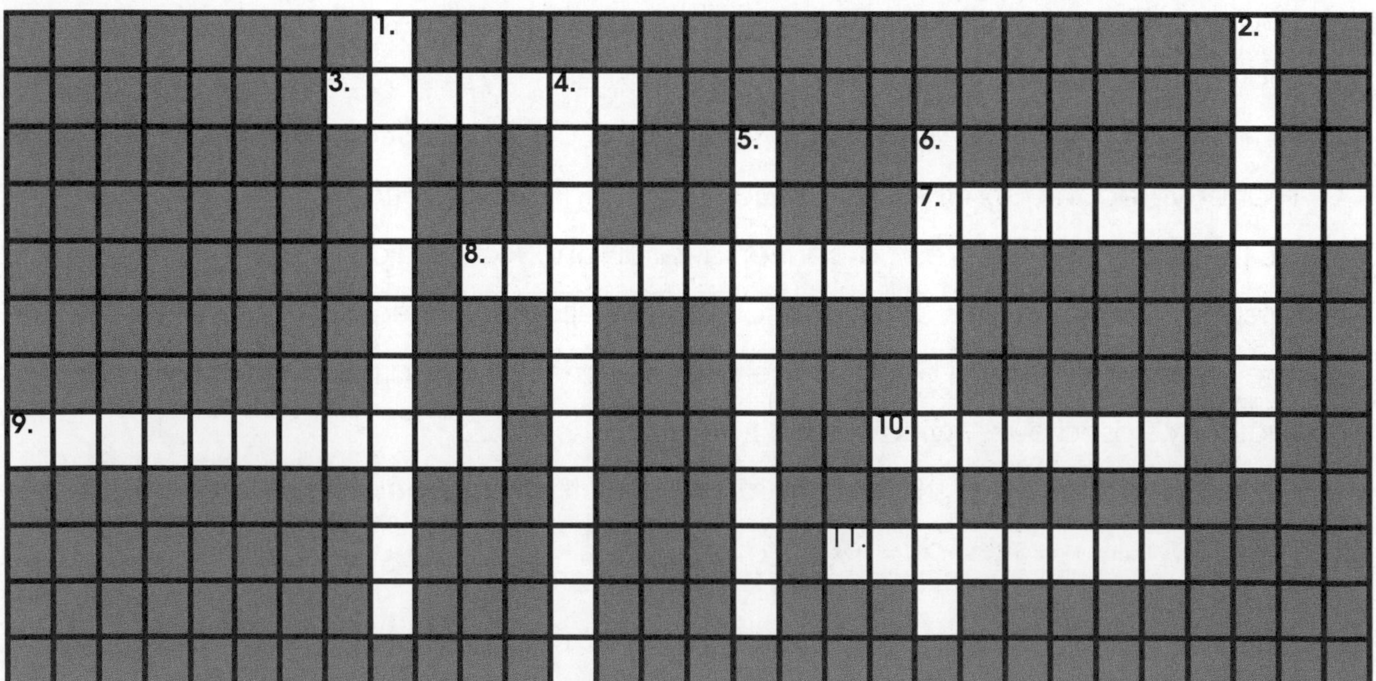

NAME ______________________

Review Prefixes and Suffixes

Use the table to help you remember the meanings of the suffixes you learned.

-sion, **-tion** = act, state, or quality of	**-ly** = in a way
-er, **-or** = a person who	**-y** = being, having
-ist = one who makes or practices	**-al**, **-ial** = having the characteristic of
-ness, **-ship** = state of being	**-ous**, **-ious** = having the quality of
-ance, **-ence** = state of being, the act of	

Read the sentences below. Replace each set of bold words with a word that contains one of the suffixes from above and write it on the line.

1. On October 29, 1929, "Black Tuesday," the stock market crashed and sent the United States into the Great **state of being depressed** ______________.
2. Everyone from **people who farm** ______________ to **people who make art** ______________ to **people who teach** ______________ suffered severe **state of being hard** ______________ during this period in history.
3. As much as 25 percent of workers were unemployed, and the **act of competing** ______________ for existing jobs was fierce.
4. People were desperate for strong **state of being a leader** ______________, and in 1932, Franklin D. Roosevelt was elected president.
5. The New Deal was the name of Roosevelt's program to combat the economic, social, and **having the characteristics of finances** ______________ effects of the Depression.
6. There is not one single **act of explaining** ______________ of why the Great Depression took place.
7. Although things were **in a slow way** ______________ starting to improve in the late 1930s, it was preparation for World War II that finally changed the economic situation.

REVIEW: CHAPTER 2 LESSONS 8–9

NAME ______________________________

Lesson 2.10 Syllabication

Words can be divided into parts called **syllables**. Each syllable has one vowel sound, so the number of a word's vowel sounds equals the number of syllables.

laugh·ing = 2 vowel sounds = 2 syllables
car·ou·sel = 3 vowel sounds = 3 syllables
o·per·a·tion = 4 vowel sounds = 4 syllables

Read the paragraphs below. Next to each bold word write the number of vowel sounds you hear when you say the word out loud.

Would ______ you ever **consider** ______ eating food grown in **manure** ______ inside a cave or a dark cellar? How do you feel about **consuming** ______ **fungus** ______? You might like **mushrooms** ______ on a pizza, but **most** ______ people give little **thought** ______ to the origins of the mushrooms they eat.

Although ______ there are many **varieties** ______ of mushrooms, only a limited number are **edible** ______. People who **forage** ______ for mushrooms in the **wild** ______ must be **exceedingly** ______ careful. About 200 species of fungi are **poisonous** ______. It's not always **easy** ______ to tell which mushrooms are **dangerous** ______. There's no **need** ______ to worry about the mushrooms you buy at the store, **however** ______. They are raised for the **purpose** ______ of selling in markets, or they are **gathered** ______ by **experienced** ______ hunters.

Truffles are the most **valuable** ______ fungi. They grow **underground** ______ and are difficult to find. **Specially**-trained ______ pigs and dogs are often **used** ______ to locate them in the wild. It's worth all the trouble, **though** ______: a pound of truffles can sell for as much as 700 **dollars** ______!

Phonics Connection
Find three bold words that contain the /ə/ sound. Write them on the lines and circle the letter or letters that make the sound.

______________________ ______________________ ______________________

NAME ____________________

Lesson 2.10 Syllabication

- A two-syllable compound word can be divided into syllables between the parts of the compound. — some·thing sail·boat
- A word that has a prefix or suffix is divided between the prefix or suffix and the base word. — **re**·place bright·**ness**
- A word that has two consonants between two vowels (VCCV) is divided between consonants. — ma**g**·**n**et e**f**·**f**ort
- If a word has the VCV pattern, listen to the first vowel sound. If it is long, the word is usually divided after the first vowel. — **o**·pen **fi**·nal
- If it is short, the word is usually divided after the consonant. — m**et**·al s**al**·ad

On the line, write the word from the box that names each picture below. Draw a slash (/) to divide the word into syllables.

hamburger lemon planets acorn grasshopper
cupcake icicles jellyfish chimney

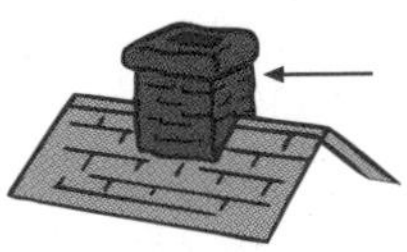

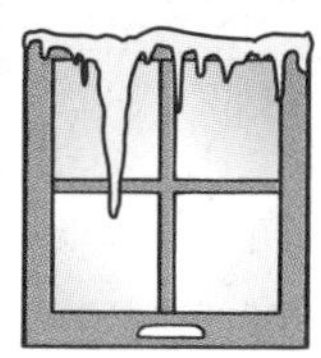

NAME ______________________________

Review Syllabication

Read the entries in the time line below. Next to each bold word, write the number of vowel sounds. Then, draw slashes to divide the word into syllables.

The History of Transportation

@ 3500 B.C.	the first wheeled carts are invented
1620	Cornelius Drebbel creates the first **submarine** ______
1662	Blaise Pascal's horse-drawn bus, the first **public** ______ bus, runs **along** ______ the streets of Paris
1769	the self-propelled **motor** ______ **vehicle** ______ is invented by Nicholas-Joseph Cugnot
1783	the first hot air **balloon** ______, manned by the Montgolfier brothers, takes to the skies
1786	the first working **steamboat** ______ in the **United** ______ States chugs down the **Delaware** ______ River
1791	modern **bicycles** ______ are invented in **Scotland** ______
1804	the steam-powered **locomotive** ______ is invented
1873	the first cable **streetcar** ______ is introduced in San Francisco
1885	Karl Benz patents the gas-engine **automobile** ______ in Germany
	two German inventors create the first motorcycle
1903	the Wright Brothers invent and fly the first **airplane** ______
1926	Robert Goddard launches the first liquid-fueled rocket
1936	the first working **helicopter** ______ is produced in Germany
1947	Charles Yeager pilots the first **supersonic** ______ plane and breaks the sound barrier at 662 miles per hour
1969	the first manned mission to the moon is **completed** ______
1970	the Boeing 747, the first jumbo jet, is created
1981	*Columbia*, the first space **shuttle** ______, is launched

NAME ____________________

Review Syllabication

Read the recipe below. Underline one-syllable bold words once and two-syllable bold words twice. Circle three-syllable bold words.

Jambalaya

2 **teaspoons** oil

$\frac{1}{2}$ pound chicken breast

7 ounces sliced **turkey** kielbasa

1 cup diced onion

1 diced green bell pepper

$\frac{1}{2}$ cup chopped **celery**

1 $\frac{1}{2}$ cups **white** rice

3 cups chicken broth

2 teaspoons paprika

$\frac{1}{4}$ teaspoon **ground** red pepper

$\frac{1}{2}$ teaspoon salt

1 teaspoon each dried **basil** and oregano

2 tablespoons tomato paste

1 can diced tomatoes with green chiles

$\frac{1}{2}$ pound cleaned, raw **shrimp**

$\frac{1}{4}$ cup chopped green **onions**

1. Cut the chicken into little pieces. (Be sure to wash your hands **thoroughly** each time you touch raw meat or **seafood**.) Heat the oil in a large **saucepan**. Cook the chicken for about five minutes, and then transfer it to another dish.
2. Add the onion, pepper, and celery to the pan. Cook, **stirring** occasionally, for about 8 minutes. Add the kielbasa, and cook for an additional 5 minutes.
3. Add the rice, broth, and **seasonings** to the vegetable **mixture**. Bring it to a **boil**, then cover it and **reduce** the heat to low. Simmer for about 15 minutes.
4. Add the chicken, **tomato** paste, and diced tomatoes, and cook for 10 minutes.
5. Add the shrimp and green onions, and cook **just** until the shrimp turn pink.
6. **Garnish** with green onions, and serve with hot sauce. Recipe **yields** 6 servings.

* **Remember**, you should always ask an **adult** for help in the kitchen when using knives or the stove.

NAME ______________________________

Lesson 3.1 Synonyms and Antonyms

- A **synonym** is a word that has the same or almost the same meaning as another word.
  supply, provide   decrease, lessen   astonish, surprise
- An **antonym** is a word that means the opposite of another word.
  complex, simple   allow, forbid   temporary, permanent

Read the sentences below. On the line, write the word from the box that is a synonym for each bold word.

probable	happen	origin	briefly	recall	quick

1. Even people who don't usually **remember** ________________ their dreams once they awaken still dream every night.
2. The majority of dreams **occur** ________________ during a type of sleep that is known as REM, or **rapid** ________________ eye movement, sleep.
3. During REM sleep, the eyes move quickly back and forth, breathing becomes faster, and the body is **temporarily** ________________ paralyzed.
4. Scientists don't agree about the **source** ________________ of dreams or their meanings.
5. Studies done on animals show that mammals and birds have sleep cycles that are similar to humans, so it is **likely** ________________ that they also dream.

Read the sets of words below. Circle the pair of antonyms in each set.

1.	compliment	correct	insult	solution
2.	question	answer	ignore	prepare
3.	worn	separate	stiff	flexible
4.	different	ancient	modern	ordinary
5.	useless	public	increase	private

NAME ________________________

Lesson 3.1 Synonyms and Antonyms

Read the paragraphs below. If the bold word is followed by an **A**, find an antonym from the box and write it on the line. If it is followed by an **S**, find a synonym and write it on the line.

finishing	always	altered	fortunately	viewpoint	group	previous
motivated	located	cowardly	vanished	failures	insignificant	

Amelia Earhart was a **courageous** (A) ________________ woman who forever **changed** (S) ________________ the world's **perspective** (S) ________________ about women in aviation.

Earhart was nationally recognized in 1928 when she became the first woman to fly across the Atlantic. However, she was only a passenger on the plane. The trip **inspired** (S) ________________ Earhart to plan a **solo** (A) ________________ transatlantic flight. Four years later, on May 20, 1932, Earhart flew across the ocean and set a record by **completing** (S) ________________ the journey in 14 hours and 56 minutes.

The **next** (A) ________________ important flight Earhart planned was the crossing of the Pacific Ocean, from Hawaii to California. Although this might not seem like a **monumental** (A) ________________ trip today, no other aviators at that time had successfully accomplished the goal. In 1935, Earhart made the trip and added another record to her list of **achievements** (A) ________________.

Amelia Earhart's next mission was to fly all the way around the world. **Unfortunately** (A) ________________, it was a goal that she didn't meet. On July 2, 1937, Earhart's plane **disappeared** (S) ________________ somewhere over the Pacific Ocean, near Howland Island. For years, people talked about what might have happened to the bold young aviator. To this day, no one is certain what became of Earhart and her navigator, Fred Noonan. The plane's wreckage was **never** (A) ________________ **found** (S) ________________, and it likely still rests somewhere on the ocean floor.

NAME ______________________________

Lesson 3.1 Synonyms and Antonyms

Read each clue below. Unscramble the bold letters beside it to find the word that matches the clue and write it on the line.

1. an antonym for *success* **ilurfae** ____________
2. a synonym for *feeble* **keaw** ____________
3. a synonym for *thin* **endsler** ____________
4. an antonym for *cautious* **aecrelss** ____________
5. a synonym for *vacant* **tyepm** ____________
6. an antonym for *awkward* **cefgraul** ____________
7. a synonym for *brave* **cuoraguseo** ____________
8. an antonym for *shrink* **xnepad** ____________
9. an antonym for *generous* **ytisng** ____________
10. a synonym for *frequent* **otenf** ____________
11. a synonym for *injure* **unwod** ____________
12. an antonym for *amateur* **ofessalprion** ____________

Read each pair of words below. If the words are synonyms, write **S** on the line. If they are antonyms, write **A** on the line.

1. even, odd ____________
2. verify, confirm ____________
3. amuse, bore ____________
4. fact, fiction ____________
5. understand, comprehend ____________
6. grateful, appreciative ____________
7. permit, refuse ____________
8. stiff, flexible ____________
9. pardon, forgive ____________
10. wild, tame ____________
11. peak, summit ____________
12. ignorant, knowledgeable ____________

NAME ______________________

Lesson 3.1 Synonyms and Antonyms

Read the paragraphs below and complete the activity that follows.

Have you ever had the opportunity to view a total solar eclipse? Some people think that this natural event is so amazing that they are willing to travel great distances to see it. A solar eclipse occurs when the moon passes directly in front of the sun. For a brief period of time, the sun's light is blocked by the moon. A total eclipse can usually be viewed only from a relatively small area on Earth, whereas a partial eclipse can often be seen from a larger area. When the moon is at its closest to Earth, it obscures the sun completely. When it is farther away, it covers only the central part of the sun, leaving a bright ring around the edges. This is called an *annular eclipse*.

Looking directly at the sun during an eclipse can cause great damage to the retina of the eye, even permanent blindness. One way to safely view a solar eclipse is to bring a glass full of dark liquid, like coffee or pop, outside with you. Position it so that you can see the eclipse reflected on its surface. The harmful light is absorbed by the beverage, but you can still see a clear image of the event.

1. In paragraph 1, find a synonym for *chance*. ______________
2. In paragraph 1, find an antonym for *artificial*. ______________
3. In paragraph 1, find a synonym for *incredible*. ______________
4. In paragraph 1, find a synonym for *totally*. ______________
5. In paragraph 1, find a synonym for *borders*. ______________
6. In paragraph 2, find an antonym for *temporary*. ______________
7. In paragraph 2, find a synonym for *mirrored*. ______________
8. In paragraph 2, find a synonym for *damaging*. ______________

NAME ______________________________

Lesson 3.2 Shades of Meaning

Even words that are synonyms may have different **shades of meaning**. It is important to use context to determine which word best completes a sentence.

Because the words *melt* and *thaw* have different shades of meaning, one word (*thaw*) better fits the following sentence.

Mr. Friedman almost forgot to *melt* the hamburgers for dinner.
Mr. Friedman almost forgot to *thaw* the hamburgers for dinner.

Read each pair of sentences below. Find the pair of words in the box that will complete the sentences. Write them on the lines, making sure that each word fits the meaning of the sentence.

separate, divide	knotted, tangled	strength, power
created, invented	clear, empty	

1. ____________________ the mess from the table before you start your homework.

   If you ____________________ your book bag, I can add it to this load of laundry.

2. Derek became ____________________ in the curtain as he tried to walk offstage.

   Mariah ____________________ the string tightly and handed the package to the mail carrier.

3. The artist ____________________ 20 new pieces of work for her first gallery show.

   Louis Braille ____________________ the Braille system of writing for people who cannot see.

4. ____________________ the students into groups of three.

   ____________________ the egg whites from the yolks, and beat them with a mixer.

5. My dad's new lawnmower has a lot more ____________________ than the old one.

   In gym, we lifted weights to test our ____________________.

NAME ___________________________

Lesson 3.2 Shades of Meaning

Read the paragraphs below. The words in parentheses have different shades of meaning. Underline the word that best completes each sentence.

The summer I turned 12, my life (changed, altered) forever. It wasn't in any of the ways you're (probably, likely) imagining. I didn't (misplace, lose) my best friend, my parents didn't win the lottery, and I didn't have to (transport, move) all the way across the country and start a new life somewhere else.

My older brother and I lived with our parents in a brick apartment building in downtown Chicago. I made (companions, friends) with an Indian family from two doors down when I was seven. Whenever I visited them, they told me (stories, fables) about life in India. Mrs. Mehta was always leaving covered plates filled with piping hot naan—a type of Indian flatbread—or spicy samosas at our door.

I knew that the Mehtas were (traveling, voyaging) to India for a month at the (completion, end) of the summer, but I had no (thought, idea) I'd be invited to join them. My parents were both working long hours that summer, and my brother had unexpectedly gotten (a job, an occupation) at the college where he would attend classes in the fall.

If I hadn't traveled halfway around the world with the Mehtas, would I still have (detected, discovered) my passion for photography? I quickly found that I loved the way I could (capture, trap) a moment on film. The colors, movement, and activity in India astounded me. I didn't want to miss anything because I knew I could never describe in words the world I was seeing.

Every few years, I join the Mehtas on their journey (home, house). I bring my camera with me, of course, because I haven't gone anywhere without it in years. I walk the streets of Bangalore, and I remember how they inspired me to discover my talent for photography the summer I turned 12.

NAME ______________________

Lesson 3.3 Levels of Specificity

Some words give the reader more detailed information than others.

- In the following set of words—*pear, fruit, food—the* word *food* is the most general. *Fruit* is a more specific type of *food.* The word *pear* is more specific than either *food* or *fruit.*

Read the sets of words below. On the line, rewrite each set in order from general to specific.

1.	collie	mammal	dog	______________________
2.	city	Las Vegas	place	______________________
3.	illness	disease	diabetes	______________________
4.	subject	language	French	______________________
5.	celebration	event	birthday	______________________
6.	panic	feeling	worry	______________________
7.	tree	willow	plant	______________________
8.	vehicle	car	sedan	______________________
9.	structure	stadium	building	______________________
10.	coin	dime	currency	______________________

Phonics Connection

Use the words above to answer the questions that follow.

1. Find one word that contains a hard and a soft **c** and one word that contains a hard and a soft **g**, and write them on the lines.

______________ ______________

2. On the lines, list the five words that contain a consonant digraph.

______________ ______________ ______________

______________ ______________

NAME ______________________

Lesson 3.3 Levels of Specificity

Read the sentences below. For each word in bold, there is a more specific word in the box. Find the word and write it on the line.

sergeant	novelist	pediatrician	teapots	fork	ballet	Orion

1. Lydia has been taking **dance** ________________ classes for three years.
2. Seamus's uncle is a **soldier** ________________ in the Marine Corps.
3. Once you know the pattern to look for, it is easy to spot the **constellation** ________________ on a clear night.
4. Please put a napkin and a **utensil** ________________ next to each guest's plate.
5. Grandma Caro has been collecting decorative **containers** ________________ for nearly half a century.
6. Xavier hopes to be a **writer** ________________ someday, while his sister, Asia, plans to be a **doctor** ________________.

Look at the pictures, and read the sentences below. On the line, write the word from the box that matches the picture and correctly completes the sentence.

flip-flop	bookcase	painting	duck	doghouse

1. A  ________________ is a type of fowl, which is a type of bird.
2. The word *shelter* is more general than  ________________.
3. The word *shoe* is more general than  ________________ but more specific than *footwear*.
4. The word *furniture* is more general than  ________________.
5. A still life is a type of  ________________, which is a type of art.

NAME ____________________

Review Synonyms, Antonyms, Shades of Meaning, and Levels of Specificity

Read the paragraphs below. On the line beside each bold word, write a synonym. On the line beside each underlined word, write an antonym.

Take a moment, and try to think of **different** ______________ ways messages and information have been sent throughout history. Letters, e-mails, the Pony Express, and telegraphs might come to mind. Chances are, however, that you never even considered a pigeon with a <u>tiny</u> ______________ tube attached to its leg.

Homing pigeons have been used for this purpose in Egypt since at least 3000 B.C. Pigeons have also been used to **carry** ______________ emergency messages in <u>many</u> ______________ other places around the world. During times of war, pigeons were a fairly **reliable** ______________ way of sending information. One pigeon, employed by the U.S. Army Signal Corps, traveled the **amazing** ______________ distance of **approximately** ______________ 2,300 miles. Other pigeons routinely traveled distances of about 1,000 miles, flying at speeds of 30 to 60 miles per hour.

Pigeons cannot be used to send messages between two <u>random</u> ______________ locations. They can't follow directions in order to <u>arrive</u> ______________ at a certain destination. Instead, these **intelligent** ______________ birds are trained to recognize a **specific** ______________ place as home. The young birds are taken <u>farther</u> ______________ away in each bout of training, and they eventually learn to find their way home from great distances.

No one is **sure** ______________ exactly how pigeons are able to find their way home from <u>unfamiliar</u> ______________ places. Much research has been done on this <u>interesting</u> ______________ phenomenon. Some scientists believe that pigeons may use Earth's magnetic field as a sort of <u>natural</u> ______________ compass. Others believe that they use landmarks, much the way people do.

NAME ____________________

Review Synonyms, Antonyms, Shades of Meaning, and Levels of Specificity

Read the sentences below. Underline the word from the pair in parentheses that best completes the sentence. On the line, write a new sentence correctly using the word you did not underline.

1. The wreckers are coming to (demolish, ruin) the old building on Tuesday.

   ____

2. Please load the (dirty, filthy) dishes into the dishwasher before you leave.

   ____

3. Americans (eat, consume) more gas each year than people living in most other countries do.

   ____

4. (Delete, Remove) the cake from the oven in half an hour.

   ____

5. Can I (use, operate) your cell phone to call my sister?

   ____

6. If you (turn, revolve) around quickly, you might still see the great blue heron standing on a log in the pond.

   ____

Draw a line to match each word in the column on the left with a more specific word from the list beside it.

1. exercise	shampoo	7. metal	tarantula
2. shellfish	gallon	8. spider	molar
3. pepper	Japanese	9. politician	biceps
4. cleanser	aerobics	10. tooth	dill
5. Asian	jalapeño	11. herb	governor
6. measurement	shrimp	12. muscles	aluminum

REVIEW: CHAPTER 3 LESSONS 1–3

NAME ______________________

Lesson 3.4 Homophones

Words that sound the same but have different spellings and meanings are called **homophones**.

> This weekend, Dad will repair the crack in the *ceiling*.
> *Sealing* the jars properly is an important step when canning fruit.

Read the pairs of clues below. On the line, write each homophone from the box next to its definition.

sore, soar	seller, cellar	boulder, bolder	flea, flee	isle, aisle
peddle, pedal	rung, wrung	build, billed	hoarse, horse	

1. more bold ______________ a large stone ______________

2. painful ______________ to fly high in the air ______________

3. a husky or throaty voice ______________ a farmyard animal ______________

4. a person who sells things ______________ a basement ______________

5. squeezed tightly ______________ the past tense of *ring* ______________

6. the past tense of *bill* ______________ to construct ______________

7. an insect that feeds on animals ______________ to run away ______________

8. a pathway ______________ an island ______________

9. to sell ______________ to ride a bike ______________

Phonics Connection

Which pair of words in the box contains two different spellings of the long **e** sound?

______________ ______________

NAME ____________________

Lesson 3.4 Homophones

Read the sentences below. Underline the word from the pair in parentheses that correctly completes each sentence.

1. It took a crew of nearly 20,000 people to (billed, build) the Taj Mahal during the 1600s.
2. The Eiffel Tower, which was completed in 1889, has been a popular (symbol, cymbal) of France for more than a century.
3. San Francisco's Coit Tower, which contains murals painted by 26 different artists, can be reached by only one (road, rode).
4. The tallest (mettle, metal) staircase in the world can be found inside Toronto's famous CN Tower.
5. Australia's Sydney Opera House is a unique piece of architecture that looks like a series of billowing (sails, sales) on boats in the harbor.
6. The United States (Capital, Capitol), located at the east end of the National Mall in Washington, D.C., houses Congress.
7. Italy's Leaning Tower of Pisa is currently about three feet taller on one (sighed, side) than the other.
8. The Great Wall of China, which stretches nearly 4,000 miles, can be (seen, scene) from outer space.

Read the pairs of homophones below. Use each word in a sentence. You may use a dictionary if you need to check the meaning of a word.

1. (chili, chilly) ____________________

____

2. (throne, thrown) ____________________

____

3. (stationary, stationery) ____________________

____

NAME ____________________

Lesson 3.5 Multiple-Meaning Words

A **multiple-meaning word**, or **homograph**, is a word that has more than one meaning. Context can help you determine which meaning the author intends.

Mary Kelly is the newest member of the law *firm*.
The tomato feels *firm*, so it is probably not ripe yet.

Read each sentence and the definitions that follow. Circle the letter of the definition that matches the bold word.

1. In October of 2003, an amazing new water **bridge** opened in Germany.

a. a card game **b.** a structure that connects two areas

2. Although the **project** was begun in the 1930s, World War II and the Cold War stopped its progress until the 1990s.

a. a task or plan **b.** to cause an image to appear on a surface

3. On the day the bridge opened, hundreds of people lined the **banks** of the Elbe River to watch the first ships pass overhead.

a. the land beside a body of water **b.** places where people keep their money

4. The bridge is 3,011 **feet** long and cost the equivalent of more than 600 million dollars to build.

a. the bottoms of legs **b.** measurements equal to 12 inches

5. Imagine how **stable** and strong the bridge must be to withstand the weight of all that water!

a. a building where horses are kept **b.** sturdy; not easily moved

6. Thousands of **pounds** of steel and concrete were used in its construction.

a. units of weight **b.** hits something over and over

NAME ____________________

Lesson 3.5 Multiple-Meaning Words

Read each sentence below. On the line, write a sentence using another meaning of the bold word. If you need help, you may use a dictionary.

1. The members of the quiz team were preparing for a **match** against their toughest competitor.

   ____

2. Their **records** were tied, and each team badly wanted to win.

   ____

3. In order to be **fair**, the questions were chosen randomly.

   ____

4. There were six **pupils** on each team, as well as two substitutes.

   ____

5. At the end of each **round**, the coaches took a few minutes to give the contestants a pep talk.

   ____

6. Although it was **kind** of difficult to concentrate in front of a crowd, most of the contestants had learned to focus their attention on the competition.

   ____

7. Winning the final match would **mean** the chance to compete in the regional championships.

   ____

8. The judges would **present** the winning team with a trophy.

   ____

Phonics Connection

1. Which bold word above contains the long **i** sound? ____________________
2. Which bold word above contains a vowel diphthong? ____________________

NAME ____________________

Review Homophones and Multiple-Meaning Words

Read the paragraphs below. On each line, write a homophone for the bold word. Some words have more than one correct answer.

Neither Kate nor Emily had ever **been** ________________ to a **flea** ________________ market before, but they knew **their** ________________ grandma went frequently. She collected antique perfume bottles, old quilts, and postcards from around the world.

"It really doesn't matter **whether** ________________ or not we **find** ________________ anything today," Grandma told the girls. "I think you'll enjoy browsing the booths and people watching."

Although it was not yet 10, the outdoor flea market was already humming with activity. Kate, Emily, and Grandma made their **way** ________________ **through** ________________ the crowd and began looking at the goods set on tables and piled in bins. The **sellers** ________________ eagerly answered questions from potential buyers.

Kate loved sifting through the old-fashioned **clothes** ________________ and imagining who their owners might have been. She held up a cheery red dress with a **flower** ________________ peeking out of the pocket. She couldn't wait to try it on.

"Did you find anything?" Emily asked, as Grandma entered the booth.

Her grandma **sighed** ________________. "I found a beautiful quilt," she said. "I could tell that each **piece** ________________ of fabric had a story to tell. I was ready to **buy** ________________ it when I noticed a **hole** ________________ in the lining. I couldn't help myself, though. I bought it anyway, but it looks like I've got some work ahead of me."

Kate smiled. "You can't fool us," she said. "We know that your favorite finds are things that **need** ________________ a little love and attention."

"You girls **know** ________________ me too well!" Grandma exclaimed.

NAME ____________________

Review Homophones and Multiple-Meaning Words

Read the paragraphs and answer the questions that follow.

No one knows for sure when or where playing cards were invented. One theory says that they were developed in India as a variation on chess. Others think that cards were first used as game markers in China or Egypt. Wherever they came from originally, they reached the Middle East about a thousand years ago and arrived in Europe during the 1200s.

Card decks in those days had to be hand drawn or painted. This process made each deck very expensive. Only wealthy people, especially royalty, played card games. Around 1400, though, wood blocks were first used to print cards, so the decks became more affordable. Today, almost three-quarters of the world's population play some sort of card games.

The deck that is most commonly used has four suits—hearts, spades, diamonds, and clubs. Each suit is made of 13 cards—king, queen, jack, ace, and cards numbered two through ten.

Cards have given artists and designers a unique outlet for their work. Some decks contain a story in pictures that runs from one card to the next. Other decks display photographs or drawings of a particular group of people or objects. For instance, one deck may show 52 vintage cars and another might show 52 British manor houses.

1. In Paragraph 2, which word means *obstructs* and *cubes*? ____________________
2. In Paragraph 3, which word means *hits* and *organizations*? ____________________
3. In Paragraph 3, which word means *knock down* and *platform*? ____________________
4. In Paragraph 4, which word means *tale* and *floor or level*? ____________________
5. In Paragraph 4, which word means *things* and *disapproves*? ____________________
6. In Paragraph 4, which word means *exit* and *plug*? ____________________

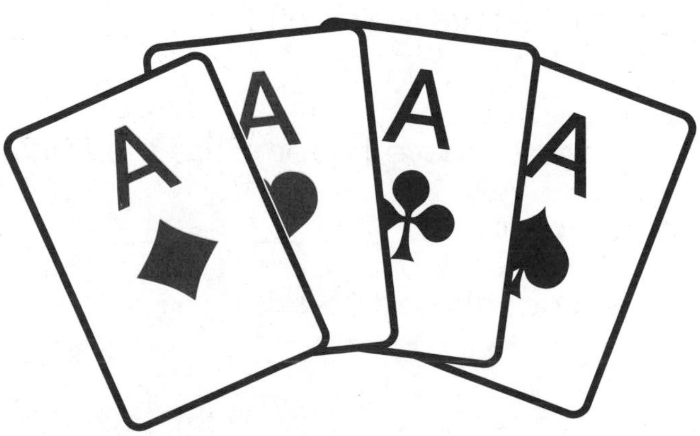

NAME ____________________

Lesson 3.6 Clipped Words and Acronyms

Clipped words are words that are commonly used in their shortened forms for convenience.

vet = veterinarian   flu = influenza   exam = examination

Jefferson Middle School is hosting an auction as a school fundraiser. Find the word in each item that can be clipped, underline it, and write the shortened form of the word on the line.

1. a one-year membership to the Wyndham Zoological Gardens ____________
2. the chance to play a game and get some tips from international tennis champion Austin Mills ____________
3. two airplane tickets to Maui, Hawaii ____________
4. one school year's worth of mathematics tutoring from the qualified tutors at the Learning Center ____________
5. a full family membership to Malleys' Gymnasium (any of our four locations) ____________
6. two courtside tickets to the professional basketball game of your choice at Wyndham Arena ____________
7. certificates redeemable for 25 free hamburgers at Whitey's Drive-Thru ____________
8. two evenings of unlimited limousine service ____________
9. a one-year pass to Mo's Miniature Golf World ____________

Phonics Connection

Use your answers from the exercise above to complete the following items.

1. Which two words contain digraphs? ____________ ____________
2. Which word contains two **r**-controlled vowels? ____________

NAME ______________________________

Lesson 3.6 Clipped Words and Acronyms

Acronyms and **initializations** are abbreviations using the first letter of each word in a name or title. In an acronym, the letters are pronounced as a word (NATO). In an initialization, the individual letters are pronounced (UN).

NATO = **N**orth **A**tlantic **T**reaty **O**rganization UN = **U**nited **N**ations

In some abbreviations, small words, like articles or prepositions, are left out.

ESL = **E**nglish as a **s**econd **l**anguage

On the line, write an acronym or initialization for each set of words.

1. unidentified flying object ______________
2. self-contained underwater breathing apparatus ______________
3. Parent-Teacher Association ______________
4. grade point average ______________
5. sports utility vehicle ______________
6. University of North Carolina ______________
7. Central Intelligence Agency ______________

Read the sentences below. On the line, write the initialization from the box that matches each bold phrase.

LOL	HAND	ASAP	OTOH	IMO	BTW

1. **In my opinion** ______________, the game lasted way too long.
2. E-mail me **as soon as possible** ______________.
3. Mr. Haas had the whole class **laughing out loud** ______________.
4. **By the way** ______________, I borrowed your blue sweater.
5. I'd like to go to the movies tonight. **On the other hand** ______________, my favorite show is on TV.
6. **Have a nice day** ______________ and don't forget your lunch!

NAME ______________________________

Lesson 3.7 Word Play

A **palindrome** is a word or sentence that reads the same forward and backward.

madam   noon   Step on no pets.   Top spot.

Circle the letter of the palindrome in each pair below.

1. a. Race fast, safe car.
   b. Roy, am I the mayor?
2. a. Stella won no wallets.
   b. Ned, I am not a maiden.
3. a. Never odd nor even.
   b. Dr. Awkward
4. a. Flee to me, my remote elf.
   b. Wontons? Not now.
5. a. Was it a car or some cat I saw?
   b. Nurses run.
6. a. Gary knits me stinky rag.
   b. Did Hannah say as Hannah did?
7. a. Too bad I've hidden a boot.
   b. Some men interpret nine memos.
8. a. A man, a plan, a canal, Panama!
   b. Don't ever nod.

An **anagram** is formed by rearranging the letters of another word.

night → thing   limped → dimple   won → now

Read the sentences below. Circle the word in each sentence that is an anagram for the bold word.

1. Maria packed three **pairs** of shoes for her trip to Paris.
2. Casey grabbed a stack of paper, a stapler, two pens, and a few **tacks**.
3. We'll need more time if we are going to visit all of the landmarks in **Rome**.
4. Dad **omits** most of the oil from the recipe, but his chocolate cake is still always moist and delicious.
5. Did you buy enough **meat** to feed everyone on the team?
6. Every March, my grandma gives me a new **charm** for my bracelet.
7. **None** of the passengers noticed the small neon sign.

NAME ______________________

Lesson 3.7 Word Play

A **portmanteau** (pôrt′ man tō′) word is a combination of two other words. Unlike a compound word, it contains only parts of the words.

bash = bang + smash　　moped = motor + pedal

Read the sentences below. Replace each set of bold words with a portmanteau word from the box.

Internet	flurry	splattered	dumbfound	scrawl
guestimated	smog	brunch	splurged	

1. After **breakfast** + **lunch** ________________, Rashid sat down at the computer.
2. He brought up the **international network** ________________ so that he could research ideas for a science fair project.
3. Rashid wanted to find something spectacular, something that would **dumb** + **confound** ________________ his entire class.
4. For the previous year's fair, he had **splashed** + **surged** ________________ on a kit he had found online.
5. It was supposed to demonstrate how **smoke** + **fog** ________________ in large cities was contributing to global warming, but it hadn't been much of a success.
6. The materials weren't very good quality, and water had **splashed** + **spattered** ________________ all over Rashid's table at the fair.
7. After scanning several sites, Rashid suddenly found the perfect idea and began to **scribble** + **sprawl** ________________ the instructions on a piece of scrap paper.
8. He **guessed** + **estimated** ________________ how much he would need of certain materials and headed to the store in a **flutter** + **hurry** ________________ of excitement.

NAME ______________________

Review Clipped Words, Acronyms, and Word Play

Read each clipped word below. Its unabbreviated form is written beside it, but the letters are scrambled. Unscramble them and write the word on the line.

1. tie → **cktinee** ______________
2. prof → **ofeporrss** ______________
3. exam → **eamionxanit** ______________
4. vet → **ianverinaret** ______________
5. sub → **stituubste** ______________
6. mini → **mniiauret** ______________
7. ref → **eerfere** ______________

REVIEW: CHAPTER 3 LESSONS 6–7

Replace each set of bold words with an acronym or an initialization.

1. Sonia made herself a **bacon, lettuce, and tomato** ______________ sandwich for lunch.
2. Mr. Jimenez filed his tax return online at the Web site for the **Internal Revenue Service** ______________.
3. Bryan's uncle was a **prisoner of war** ______________ during the Gulf War.
4. "Tell your sister to hurry because we have to leave **as soon as possible** ______________."
5. Our **video cassette recorder** ______________ is broken, but we usually watch DVDs anyway.
6. After graduating from high school, William will attend the **Massachusetts Institute of Technology** ______________.
7. When you see the French phrase ***Respondez s'il vous plait*** ______________ on an invitation, you should let the host know whether you'll be attending the event.
8. **The North Atlantic Treaty Organization** ______________ has its headquarters in Brussels, Belgium, and was established in 1949.

NAME ______________________

Review Clipped Words, Acronyms, and Word Play

Read the sentences and phrases below. On the line, write the word from the box that correctly completes each palindrome. You may want to use a piece of scrap paper to help you figure out which word is missing.

race	tell	save	frost	drawn

1. We'll let Dad ______________ Lew.
2. A tip: ______________ Eva's pita.
3. Are we not ______________ onward to new era?
4. Anne, I vote more cars ______________ Rome to Vienna.
5. No mists or ______________, Simon.

On the line, write the letter of the word in column 2 that is an anagram for each word in column 1.

1. ______________	ocean	a. dusty
2. ______________	saint	b. Madison
3. ______________	study	c. canoe
4. ______________	west	d. stain
5. ______________	domains	e. dense
6. ______________	needs	f. stew

Use the words in the box to solve the problems below.

Medicare	fourteen	gleam	twirl

1. medicine + care = ______________
2. ______________ + nights = fortnight
3. twist + whirl = ______________
4. ______________ + shimmer = glimmer

REVIEW: CHAPTER 3 LESSONS 6–7

NAME ______________________________

Lesson 3.8 Figures of Speech

A **simile** is a comparison of two unlike things using the words *like* or *as*.

The *row of trees stood* along the driveway, *like soldiers at attention.*
The surface of the *table* was *as slick and shiny as a newly frozen pond.*

Read the paragraphs below and underline the seven similes.

The day of the Sixth Annual Delridge Kite Festival was crisp and clear with a light steady breeze. The sky was as perfectly blue as the inside of a swimming pool, and the Jiangs gulped deep breaths of fresh ocean air. For the first hour, they wandered the festival, absorbing the sights and sounds like sponges. They stopped to watch an older man wearing a bright red baseball cap as he prepared his enormous octopus kite for flight. His face, browned from the sun, was as creased as a walnut, and he paused to smile at the family before he continued his preparations.

The man was more than happy to discuss his hobby with the Jiangs, and they stayed to watch the octopus catch the breeze and inflate like a balloon. The kite's handler jogged along beneath the wild sea creature, deftly moving the strings like a puppeteer working a marionette.

There was a kite-making booth for children at one end of the park, so Max and Victoria spent about an hour crafting their own kites from heavyweight paper, dowel rods, and twine. Around noon, the Jiangs retrieved their cooler from the van. They found an empty picnic table and ate with their heads tilted backward as the kite ballet began.

A group of nearly a hundred kites filled the sky like bits of brightly-colored confetti. As each kite caught the wind, it soared effortlessly, like a hawk riding a current with outstretched wings. Slowly the kites moved into formation and began a graceful dance. The Jiangs exchanged looks of amazement and then returned their gaze to the performance in the sky.

NAME ________________________

Lesson 3.8 Figures of Speech

A **metaphor** is a comparison of two unlike things without using *like* or *as*.

The *buttercups* were *a colorful blanket* spread across the yard.

On the lines, tell which two things in each metaphor are being compared.

1. The leaves of the seedlings were tiny hands reaching toward the sun.

   ____________________ ____________________

2. The three golf balls Preston found were perfectly round eggs nestled in the high grasses beside the pond.

   ____________________ ____________________

3. Once the Nelsons lost power, their house quickly became an icebox.

   ____________________ ____________________

4. The little white dog's tail was a flag waving proudly in spite of the rain.

   ____________________ ____________________

5. For the kids, the seashells were tiny treasures strewn along the beach.

   ____________________ ____________________

6. When Davis put on his hockey uniform, he became a warrior heading into battle.

   ____________________ ____________________

7. The lights of the city were a constellation speckling the night sky.

   ____________________ ____________________

Phonics Connection

On the lines, write four words from the exercise above that contain the diphthongs **ou** or **ow**. ____________________ ____________________

____________________ ____________________

NAME ______________________________

Lesson 3.8 Figures of Speech

Personification, which is a type of figurative language, means *to give human characteristics to animals or objects.*

> The sun winked slyly at the moon just before it sank below the horizon.
> The train wrapped itself lazily around the curvy mountain tracks.

In both examples above, objects (the sun and the train) are given human qualities (*winking slyly* and *wrapping lazily*).

Read the sentences below. Underline the word or words that indicate the sentence is an example of personification.

1. The stooped sunflowers dance with one another in the cool morning breeze.
2. The rays of the morning sun skip joyfully into Sierra's bedroom.
3. The mole looked anxiously at his watch before scurrying across the lawn and shimmying into a hole he had dug early that morning.
4. The bright red maple leaf sighed sorrowfully as it drifted to the ground.
5. The night wind whistled through the trees, calling for a friend to wake up and play.
6. The last piece of chocolate cake beckoned invitingly to Rachel.
7. The moped coughed and sputtered, gasping for breath as its engine died.
8. The camera eagerly captured each moment, tucking it away for another day.
9. The wind angrily rattled the windows, but they refused to open.
10. The chickadees perched in the branches of the old willow tree bickered loudly with one another.

On the lines below, write your own examples of personification. Remember, you can personify anything that is not human.

1. ____

2. ____

NAME ____________________

Lesson 3.8 Figures of Speech

Read the following paragraphs. Underline the eight similes and circle the two metaphors.

As Juan and his father neared the lake, the paved road disappeared and two strips of gravel became their guide. The crunch of the truck's tires across the rocks was like someone digging into a bag of potato chips. Suddenly, Juan was hungry for lunch, even though it was only ten in the morning.

The four-hour drive from home to the lake had flown by like school recess, mostly because Juan was having so much fun. He and his dad jammed the radio, talked about sports, and carried on like a couple of old fishing buddies. This trip was only their second time out to the lake, but in some ways it felt like they'd been doing it forever.

Soon, the boat drifted quietly through the fog like a leaf bobbing along atop the waves. Juan's dad didn't say much. He was now a sea captain hunting for the best spot to drop anchor. Every few minutes, Juan asked if they could cast their lines yet. His dad told him that he sounded like a broken record.

Finally, Juan's dad steered the boat into a small area surrounded by foliage. All along the banks, tree branches hung down into the water. They looked like divers frozen at the moment they hit the surface.

Juan took a pole from his dad and smiled in anticipation. Then, he cast his line into the water as if he had been asked to throw the first pitch at a baseball game—the honor was more important than actually hitting the plate.

Before he knew it, though, Juan had a bite. The line became a laser beam cutting straight through the water's surface. Juan's dad told him to slowly reel the line in, a few turns at a time. Like pulling a bucket from a well, he lifted the fish out of the water and into the boat. Juan knew his lunch would be more than a bag of potato chips now.

NAME ______________________

Lesson 3.9 Idioms

A group of words that mean something other than what they appear to mean is called an **idiom**. In the sentence that follows, the idiom *get the ball rolling* means that things are getting started.

> Although the deadline was still two months away, Vicente and Erica decided to *get the ball rolling* early.

Read each idiom and definition below. On the line that follows, write a sentence using the idiom.

1. got up on the wrong side of the bed = to be in a bad mood or to have started the day out badly

   ____

2. pull your own weight = to do your share

   ____

3. cost an arm and a leg = to be very expensive

   ____

4. go the extra mile = to go out of one's way to be helpful or to do a good job

   ____

5. give someone a hand = to be helpful

   ____

6. under the weather = feeling ill

   ____

7. keep your chin up = to try to stay cheerful, even in a difficult situation

   ____

8. steal the spotlight = receive all the attention

   ____

NAME ______________________

Lesson 3.9 Idioms

Underline the idiom in each sentence below.

1. Daniel made a beeline from his school to the library.
2. If he was quick enough, getting a computer would be a piece of cake.
3. Once other students arrived, he wouldn't have a fighting chance of getting online until after four o'clock.
4. He knew he couldn't just sail through the rest of the semester without working.
5. Daniel was all thumbs as he fumbled with his bike lock.
6. Daniel couldn't believe his eyes when he saw the sign that said the computers were down.
7. At first, he felt completely down in the dumps.
8. Then, he remembered that a librarian named Mr. Hernandez had bent over backwards helping him in the past.
9. In the blink of an eye, Daniel found himself working on a computer in the adult section, thanks to Mr. Hernandez.

Now, write each idiom next to its definition on the lines provided.

reasonable possibility of success ______________________

depressed or sad ______________________

straight or direct route ______________________

tried very hard ______________________

clumsy ______________________

easy ______________________

very quickly ______________________

see something unbelievable ______________________

get through something easily ______________________

NAME ______________________________

Lesson 3.10 Analogies

An **analogy** shows a relationship between two pairs of words. To understand an analogy, it is important to figure out how the words relate to one another.

- *Bored* is to *excited* as *wide* is to *narrow*.
  Bored is an antonym for *excited* as *wide* is an antonym for *narrow*.
- *Wheel* is to *car* as *page* is to *book*.
  A wheel is part of a car, just as a page is part of a book.
- *Bird* is to *nest* as *horse* is to *stable*.
  A nest is the home of a bird, just as a stable is the home of a horse.

To read an analogy written in the following format—puppy : dog :: lamb : sheep—you would say, "*Puppy* is to *dog* as *lamb* is to *sheep*."

The analogies below are incomplete. Underline the word from the pair in parentheses that best completes each analogy.

1. (Increase, Reduce) is to *decrease* as *question* is to *answer*.
2. *Sprinkle* is to *sprinkling* as (copied, copy) is to *copying*.
3. *Mitten* is to *hand* as *sock* is to (finger, foot).
4. *Nickel* is to *dollar* as (second, hour) is to *minute*.
5. (Never, Often) is to *frequently* as *vanish* is to *disappear*.
6. (September, March) is to *April* as *breakfast* is to *lunch*.
7. *Athlete* is to *team* as (student, principal) is to *class*.
8. *Eight* is to *ate* as *carats* is to (carrots, vegetables).
9. *Refrigerator* is to (food, stove) as *closet* is to *clothing*.
10. *Vacuum* is to (sponge, cleaning) as *trowel* is to *gardening*.
11. *Forty-two* is to (twenty-four, twenty-two) as *sixty-one* is to *sixteen*.
12. *Ballet* is to *dance* as *piano* is to (trombone, instrument).
13. *Lemon* is to *sour* as *chocolate* is to (sweet, cake).

NAME ______________________

Lesson 3.10 Analogies

Replace each picture below with a word that correctly completes the analogy.

1. *Moo* is to  ______________ as *hiss* is to *snake*.

2. *Adult* is to  ______________ as *butterfly* is to *caterpillar*.

3. *Freeze* is to 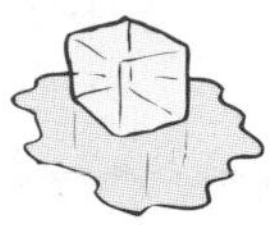 ______________ as *ancient* is to *modern*.

4. 

______________ is to *temperature* as *scale* is to *weight*.

5. *Wisconsin* is to  ______________ as *star* is to *constellation*.

6.  ______________ is to *heat* as *windmill* is to *energy*.

Read each analogy below. Unscramble the bold word and write it on the line to complete the analogy.

1. **neegr** ______________ is to *go* as *red* is to *stop*.
2. *Nutmeg* is to **esicp** ______________ as *shrimp* is to *shellfish*.
3. **terctimeen** ______________ is to *meter* as *inch* is to *foot*.
4. *Prophet* is to **tpofir** ______________ as *oar* is to *ore*.
5. *Quill* is to *porcupine* as **eelend** ______________ is to *pincushion*.
6. *Two* is to **dboleu** ______________ as *three* is to *triple*.
7. *President* is to *country* as *mayor* is to **tyic** ______________.
8. *Armor* is to *knight* as **lshle** ______________ is to *turtle*.
9. *Flight attendant* is to **anearpli** ______________ as *chef* is to *kitchen*.
10. *Bud* is to *bloom* as *egg* is to **icechkn** ______________.

NAME ______________________________

Lesson 3.10 Analogies

Complete each analogy below with a word from the box. Remember to figure out how the words are related before you look for the missing word.

web	seedling	sport	princess	lead	patients	Detroit	bracelet

1. New Mexico : state :: ____________________ : city
2. cards : game :: basketball : ____________________
3. ____________________ : mislead :: zero : subzero
4. king : queen :: prince : ____________________
5. spider : ____________________ :: architect : house
6. ____________________ : plant :: fall : winter
7. earring : ear :: ____________________ : wrist
8. ____________________ : patience :: sundae : Sunday

Read each analogy below. Decide which category in the box it matches and write the letter of the category on the line.

a. Part–Whole Relationship	**d.** Grammatical Relationship
b. Object–Use Relationship	**e.** Object–Place Relationship
c. Numerical Relationship	**f.** Synonym or Antonym Relationship

1. _____ *Cactus* is to *desert* as *skier* is to *mountain.*
2. _____ *Slice* is to *pizza* as *button* is to *shirt.*
3. _____ *Attract* is to *repel* as *generous* is to *stingy.*
4. _____ *Book* is to *library* as *judge* is to *courthouse.*
5. _____ *Geese* is to *goose* as *marshmallows* is to *marshmallow.*
6. _____ *Seventy-three* is to *seventy-five* as *seventy-nine* is to *eighty-one.*
7. _____ *Scissors* is to *cut* as *mirror* is to *reflect.*

NAME ____________________

Lesson 3.10 Analogies

Read each analogy below. On the line, explain how the words are related.

Ex.: *Stallion* is to *horse* as *gander* is to *goose*.
A stallion is a male horse, just as a gander is a male goose.

1. *Sandpaper* is to *rough* as *silk* is to *smooth*.

____

2. *Thin* is to *slender* as *error* is to *mistake*.

____

3. *Pedal* is to *bicycle* as *hand* is to *clock*.

____

4. *Cupboard* is to *dishes* as *toolbox* is to *wrench*.

____

5. *Eighteen* is to *nine* as *twenty-six* is to *thirteen*.

____

6. *Stair* is to *stare* as *towed* is to *toad*.

____

Write three analogies of your own using the instructions that follow.

1. Write an analogy in which the words are antonyms.

____

2. Write an analogy that shows a numerical relationship.

____

3. Write an analogy that shows a grammatical relationship (such as plurals, affixes, endings, etc.). ____________________

NAME ______________________

Review Figures of Speech, Idioms, and Analogies

Read each sentence below. If it contains a metaphor, circle **M**. If it contains a simile, circle **S**.

1. **M S** The geese flew in perfect formation, as though they were bound by an invisible string.
2. **M S** The clock was an impatient observer, tapping its toes as it waited for Jake to make his move.
3. **M S** Sadie heard a sound like bacon sizzling in a frying pan, and then the phone line went dead.
4. **M S** The leaves were tiny parachutes that floated gently to the ground.
5. **M S** Fear was a mountain that towered over Will.
6. **M S** Minh closed her eyes while a cool breeze washed over her like a wave in the ocean.
7. **M S** Aidan's unspoken wish hung in the air like a balloon.
8. **M S** Cameron ignored the cheers of the crowd and listened only to the steady thump of the basketball, ringing in his ears like an ancient drumbeat.
9. **M S** Mr. Rapinski tried to start the car, but it was a grumpy child who refused to budge from the driveway.
10. **M S** The rustle of papers, like crisp leaves on a windy autumn day, was the only sound in the classroom.

On the lines below, write comparisons based on the given instructions.

1. Write a simile that includes something from nature.

____

2. Write a metaphor that includes something in your classroom.

____

3. Make a comparison using personification.

____

NAME ____________________

Review Figures of Speech, Idioms, and Analogies

Draw a line to match each idiom in column 1 to its definition in column 2.

1. hit the nail on the head	do your share
2. turn one's stomach	to study
3. take something lying down	to relax and unwind
4. hit the books	to feel disgusted by something
5. let off steam	take shortcuts
6. pull your weight	to accept something without a fight
7. cut corners	to pinpoint something exactly

The following analogies are out of order. Use the hints in line 2 of each analogy to help you place the words in the correct order.

1. *Nephew* is to *niece* as *aunt* is to *uncle*.

   ____________________ is to *niece* as ____________________ is to *nephew*.

2. *Court* is to *field* as *tennis* is to *baseball*.

   ____________________ is to *tennis* as *field* is to ____________________.

3. *Wheel* is to *rectangle* as *circle* is to *television*.

   ____________________ is to *circle* as *television* is to ____________________.

4. *Matt* is to *Jennifer* as *Jenny* is to *Matthew*.

   Matt is to ____________________ as ____________________ is to *Jennifer*.

5. *Attract* is to *illustration* as *attraction* is to *illustrate*.

   Attract is to ____________________ as ____________________ is to *illustration*.

6. *Circus* is to *theater* as *actress* is to *clown*.

   Clown is to ____________________ as *actress* is to ____________________.

REVIEW: CHAPTER 3 LESSONS 8–10

NAME ______________________________

Lesson 4.1 Guide Words and Entry Words

Guide words tell you the first and last word on a dictionary page. If the word you are searching for comes between the guide words in alphabetical order, it will appear on that page of the dictionary.

For example, *objective* might appear on a page with the guide words *obey* and *observatory*. *Kneepad* would be found with the guide words *kinship* and *knight*.

Read the following sentences. Circle the letter beside the pair of guide words that would be found on the same dictionary page as the bold word.

1. The La Brea Tar Pits are located in Los Angeles, California, in an **area** known as the Miracle Mile.

   a. architecture • armadillo **b.** aristocrat • around

2. The pits **ooze** asphalt, a sticky substance that has trapped a variety of organisms throughout history.

   a. opaque • oppose **b.** onion • opera

3. The tar pits are famous for the **extraordinary** specimens of fossilized plants, animals, and insects that have been found there.

   a. extend • extreme **b.** explode • extinct

4. Bison, mammoths, saber-toothed cats, dire wolves, and **mastodons** are among the mammals that have been found in the pits.

   a. matchbook • mature **b.** massive • matinee

5. Scientists have dated the oldest **specimen** at about 40,000 years of age.

   a. spare • species **b.** specimen • spelling

6. The oozing **asphalt** continues to occasionally trap plants and animals today.

   a. ash • aspen **b.** asparagus • assist

7. The George C. Page Museum contains more than three **million** items.

   a. mildew • millionaire **b.** millipede • mineral

NAME ____________________

Lesson 4.1 Guide Words and Entry Words

When you look up a word in a dictionary, you are looking up an **entry word.** Entry words, which are usually printed in bold, are often base words. For example, you would look for *pretty*, not *prettier*, and *silly*, not *silliness.*

entry word | pronunciation & syllables | part of speech | meaning

laboratory (lab′ rə tȯr′ ē) *noun* a room in which scientific research and experiments are done

Write the entry word beside each bold word below.

1. **crickets** ____________
2. **contains** ____________
3. **rubbing** ____________
4. **dragonflies** ____________
5. **divided** ____________
6. **mosquitoes** ____________
7. **found** ____________
8. **soaring** ____________

Use the dictionary entries below to answer the questions that follow.

sincere (sin sêr′) *adj.* honest; genuine, *noun* sincerity

squash (skwosh) **1.** *noun* a fruit that is related to pumpkins and gourds
2. *verb* to crush or press flat

refrigerator (ri frij′ ə rā′ tər) *noun* a machine or appliance that keeps food cold

1. On the line below, write a sentence using the word *squash* as a verb.

   ____

2. Which is an entry word—*sincere* or *sincerity*? ____________
3. Which guide words would you find on the same page as *refrigerator*?

   reef • refresh   reflection • regal   refugee • rehearse ____________
4. How many syllables are there in *refrigerator*? ____________

NAME ______________________

Lesson 4.2 Word Families

A **word family** is a group of words that have the same base word. Prefixes, suffixes, and endings can be added to a base word to create word families.

base word: **appoint**—**appoint**ed, **appoint**ment, dis**appoint**, dis**appoint**ment
base word: **imagine**—**imagin**ation, **imagin**ing, un**imagin**able, **imagin**ary

Read the clues below. Each clue is followed by three words from the same word family. Circle the letter of the word that matches the clue.

1. without doubt

a. doubtless **b.** doubtful **c.** doubting

2. one who studies biology

a. biological **b.** biologist **c.** biologically

3. more cheery

a. cheeriest **b.** cheerier **c.** cheerfully

4. not healthy

a. healthful **b.** healthier **c.** unhealthy

Create four word families by writing each word from the box under the correct heading.

actor	disbelief	inadmissible	creation	believable	admitting
recreation	action	creativity	reacting	unbelieving	admission

act	create	believe	admit
______	______	______	______
______	______	______	______
______	______	______	______

Phonics Connection

Which two words in the second exercise contain different spellings of the /sh/ sound?

______________ ______________

NAME ____________________

Lesson 4.2 Word Families

Read the interview below. Think of a word in the same word family as each bold word and write it on the line. Try not to use base words, when possible.

Ryan Blake: First, I'd like to know how you came up with the idea of **beginning** ________________ your own **charitable** ________________ organization.

Aliyah Howard: I was watching the news one night and saw a story about a local food pantry. The **director** ________________ was **requesting** ________________ donations. I wanted to **help** ________________, but it took a few days for my idea to take **shape** ________________.

RB: Who **assisted** ________________ you in the early stages of planning?

AH: I wouldn't have made much **progress** ________________ at all without the help of my friends Jess and Anthony, my brother Jarrod, and my dad.

RB: I know that much of the food you donate comes from your dad's restaurant. How does that **work** ________________?

AH: So much food is **wasted** ________________ every day, and I wanted to find a way to put it to good **use** ________________.

RB: How did other restaurants become involved?

AH: Jess **suggested** ________________ that we call other restaurants and bakeries in the neighborhood to see if they'd be willing to donate.

RB: What lessons do you **feel** ________________ you've learned?

AH: Everyone has the ability to make a change. You just need to be hopeful and **believe** ________________ in what you're tying to accomplish.

NAME ______________________________

Review Guide Words, Entry Words, and Word Families

Read the paragraphs below. On the line beside each bold word, write the entry word you would look for in a dictionary.

You may not know who Noah Webster was, but you are probably familiar with his life's work—the first truly American dictionary. Webster, who always had a passion for **learning** ____________________, **attended** ____________________ college at Yale University. He had hoped to continue his education at law school, but his family was not able to afford it. Instead, Webster **became** ____________________ a schoolteacher. He **wrote** ____________________ his own textbook, which was used in American **classrooms** ____________________ for more than a century.

Webster **began** ____________________ **noticing** ____________________ that Americans pronounced and spelled words in many different ways. He **thought** ____________________ that there should be more uniformity to American English and that it **shouldn't** ____________________ be exactly the same as British English. Webster's solution was to write his own dictionary—a dictionary that would be **uniquely** ____________________ American.

Webster did not take this task **lightly** ____________________. He **spent** ____________________ many years and lots of money **researching** ____________________ the origins of words. He gained a working knowledge of approximately 20 languages. He also changed the **spellings** ____________________ and pronunciations of certain words so that the American form would differ from the British. For example, he changed the spelling of *colour* to *color*, *musick* to *music*, and *plough* to *plow*. In addition, he added thousands of words that had never **appeared** ____________________ in an American dictionary.

It took Noah Webster 27 years to complete *An American Dictionary of the English Language*. It **contained** ____________________ about 70,000 **entries** ____________________ and is one of the best-selling books of all time.

REVIEW: CHAPTER 4 LESSONS 1-2

NAME ______________________

Review Guide Words, Entry Words, and Word Families

Look up each of the bold words in a dictionary. On the lines, write the guide words from the page on which you found the word.

1. **retirement** ______________ ______________
2. **beneficial** ______________ ______________
3. **aqua** ______________ ______________
4. **haunch** ______________ ______________
5. **vaccine** ______________ ______________

One member of each word family listed below is not a real word. Circle the word in each group that does not belong. Then, write the base word for each family on the line. If you need help, you may use a dictionary.

1. unexperienced	experiencing	experiential	______________
2. misalign	alignment	realignible	______________
3. regularity	irregularness	regulation	______________
4. degreased	greasy	ungreasiest	______________
5. unshipped	misshippers	shipments	______________
6. reshapement	misshapen	unshaped	______________
7. misunderstatement	restating	understated	______________
8. subdivided	divisionalness	indivisibility	______________
9. semicouraged	encouraging	courageousness	______________
10. unemployment	employingest	underemployed	______________
11. naturalistic	supernaturally	naturing	______________
12. unneeded	reneeding	neediest	______________
13. reapproving	disapproval	unapproved	______________
14. misquoting	unquoted	prequotation	______________

REVIEW: CHAPTER 4 LESSONS 1–2

NAME ______________________

Lesson 4.3 Frequently Used Foreign Words

Many words in the English language have been adopted from foreign languages. For example, *banana* is an African word, *frankfurter* is a German word, and *bronco* is a Spanish word.

Read each clue below. Choose the word from the box that matches the clue and write it on the line. Then, find the words in the word search puzzle. Words may be written forward, backward, or diagonally.

ballet	cosmonaut	origami	cello	pajamas	adios	bagel	pumpernickel

1. an Italian word for an instrument related to the violin ______________
2. a German word for a heavy dark bread ______________
3. a Russian word for *astronaut* ______________
4. a Spanish word for *good-bye* or *farewell* ______________
5. a Japanese word that describes the art of paper folding ______________
6. an East Indian word for clothes worn for sleeping ______________
7. a Yiddish word for a doughnut-shaped type of bread ______________
8. a French word for a classical form of dance ______________

h	j	l	e	k	c	i	n	r	e	p	m	u	p
e	r	m	f	b	b	g	k	o	l	a	l	p	e
v	o	e	r	y	a	b	n	a	s	j	c	x	o
o	r	l	r	y	g	l	b	z	a	a	s	y	i
m	i	v	l	p	e	d	l	q	x	m	z	u	m
e	g	a	q	f	l	i	g	e	b	a	r	y	e
j	a	y	d	r	m	n	a	l	t	s	p	w	w
k	m	h	u	i	e	x	b	m	i	r	q	m	a
n	i	t	j	a	o	l	l	e	c	b	d	s	u
s	d	g	e	c	o	s	m	o	n	a	u	t	y

NAME ______________________

Lesson 4.3 Frequently Used Foreign Words

Look up each bold word in a dictionary. On the line beside the word, write the foreign language of origin. Read the definition and then write a sentence correctly using the word.

1. **delicatessen** ______________

____

2. **ranch** ______________

____

3. **pastrami** ______________

____

4. **bouquet** ______________

____

5. **judo** ______________

____

6. **carnival** ______________

____

7. **boomerang** ______________

____

8. **yogurt** ______________

____

Phonics Connection

1. Which two bold words contain digraphs?

______________ ______________

2. In which two words is the /ü/ sound spelled differently?

______________ ______________

NAME ______________________________

Lesson 4.4 Word Histories

When you look up a word in the dictionary, you can often find the **etymology**, or **word history** listed after the definition. Word histories trace the development of words over time. In most dictionaries, the language or country of origin listed first is the most recent.

> **ignore** (ig nȯr′) *verb* to pay no attention to something (from French *ignorer*, from Latin *ignōrāre*)

Read the dictionary definitions and etymologies below, and then answer the questions that follow.

poem (pō′ əm) *noun* a piece of writing in which the words are chosen for their sounds and their meanings; often rhyming (from French *poème*, from Latin *poēma*, from Greek *poiēma*, from *poiein, create*)

tornado (tȯr nā′ dō) *noun* a severe storm with very high winds and a funnel-shaped cloud (from Spanish *tronada, thunderstorm*, from *tronar, to thunder*, from Latin *tonāre*)

umbrella (əm brel′ ə) *noun* a device that protects its user from rain or sun; usually made of cloth that covers a collapsible frame (from Italian *ombrella*, from Latin *umbrella*, influenced by *umbra, shade*)

1. Which word is Italian in origin? ______________

2. What does the Spanish word *tronada* mean? ______________

3. On the line, write the languages from which the word *poem* originates in order from oldest to most recent.

   ____

4. What does the Greek word *poiein* mean? ______________ How do you think this meaning relates to the word *poem*?

   ____

5. What Latin word is part of the word *umbrella*? ______________

NAME ______________________

Lesson 4.4 Word Histories

Read each etymology below. On the line, write the letter of the word that matches the etymology.

1. _____ from Middle English *rosten*, from Old French *rostir*
2. _____ from Latin *persuādēre, to urge*
3. _____ from Middle English *memorie*, from Anglo-French, from Latin *memoria*
4. _____ from French *toilette*, from Old French *tellette*
5. _____ from Middle English *misterie*, from Latin *mystērium*, from Greek *mustērion*
6. _____ from Native American (Massachusett) *skunk*
7. _____ from French *exclamer*, from Latin *exclāmāre*
8. _____ from Yiddish *klots*, from German *kloz, block* or *lump*
9. _____ from Greek *auto* and French *mobile* (from Latin *mobilis, to move*)
10. _____ from Italian *balcone*, of Germanic descent
11. _____ from Latin *appretiare, to appraise*

a. toilet
b. exclaim
c. mystery
d. automobile
e. klutz
f. roast
g. balcony
h. appreciate
i. memory
j. persuade
k. skunk

Look up each word in a dictionary. On the line, write the word's etymology.

1. educate ______________________
2. oxygen ______________________
3. serpent ______________________
4. plastic ______________________
5. curious ______________________
6. zero ______________________
7. continent ______________________
8. Fahrenheit ______________________

NAME ______________________

Review Frequently Used Foreign Words and Word Histories

Read the following sentences. One word in each sentence has been replaced by the name of the country or region from which it originated. Choose the correct foreign word from the box and write it on the line.

sled	carnival	potatoes	kangaroo	jungle
debris	magazine	typhoon	sherbet	pickle

1. The cool, refreshing (Turkey) slid down the back of my throat, tasting much tarter than the ice cream I had eaten yesterday. ______________
2. Bounding across the grassy plain, a (Australia) glanced about to be sure no dingoes lingered nearby. ______________
3. As Dawn waited impatiently for her mother to arrive, she flipped quickly through a (Arabia). ______________
4. The hero had to slash her way through the thick leaves and branches of the (India) to find the hidden stone ruins. ______________
5. Mikela loved eating baked (Spain) with sour cream. ______________
6. The deli always included a (Holland) and a bag of potato chips with every sandwich. ______________
7. Whenever enough snow has fallen, the Reynolds' twins take turns riding a (Dutch) down the hill in their backyard. ______________
8. The palm trees appeared to pull right out of the ground as the (China) swept across the island. ______________
9. After the storm, (France) littered the neighborhood equally from one block to the next. ______________
10. The school (Italy) had rides, games, food, and, best of all, a booth where we could throw whipped-cream pies at our teachers. ______________

NAME ______________________

Review Frequently Used Foreign Words and Word Histories

Read the dictionary entries below, and answer the questions that follow.

grumble (grum' bəl) *verb* to complain, fuss, or mutter (probably from Dutch *grommelen, to mutter*)

melody (mel' ə dē) *noun* an arrangement of sounds; a pleasant tune (from Middle English *melodie*, from Old French, from Latin *melōdia*, from Greek *melidi, singing*)

1. What does *grommelen* mean in Dutch? ______________

2. On the line, write the languages from which the word *melody* originates in order from oldest to most recent.

   ____

3. What is the Greek word for *singing*? ______________ How do you think it relates to the word *melody*?

   ____

Replace each etymology below with the word from the box it matches.

cookie	elevate	acrobat	perfume

1. Bryson bought Mom some (French *parfum*, from Old Italian *parfumo*, from *parfumare, fill with smoke*) ______________ for her birthday.

2. Kerry packed a sandwich, an orange, and a (Dutch *koekje*, meaning *little cake*, from Middle Dutch *koeke*) ______________ for lunch.

3. When Lucy sprained her ankle, the doctor told her to put ice on it and (Middle English *elevaten*, from Latin *ēlevāre*) ______________ it.

4. Julio's little brother loves to climb on things, so his dad jokes that he will grow up to be an (French *acrobate*, from Greek *akrobats*, meaning *high walker*) ______________.

Phonics Connection

Which words from the box contain the schwa sound?

______________ ______________ ______________

REVIEW: CHAPTER 4 LESSONS 3–4

NAME ______________________________

Lesson 4.5 Greek Roots

Many words in the English language have **Greek roots**. Learning the meanings of these roots can help you determine the meanings of some unfamiliar words.

chron = time	(**chron**ic)	**man** = hand	(**man**uscript)
bio = life	(**bio**logy)	**cycl** = circle, ring	(**cycl**one)
phon = sound	(tele**phon**e)	**therm** = heat	(**therm**al)

Read the clues below. Choose the word from the box that matches each clue, and write it on the line.

biography	thermos	homophones	manual	tricycle	chronological	Cyclops

1. arranged by order of time ______________
2. words that sound the same but are spelled differently ______________
3. the story of a person's life ______________
4. a vehicle that has three circular wheels ______________
5. to do something by hand ______________
6. a bottle that keeps liquids hot ______________
7. a creature from Greek mythology that has one round eye ______________

Read the sentences below. Underline the word from the pair in parentheses that correctly completes each sentence.

1. Beachwood Middle School won an award for (cycling, recycling) more materials than any other school in the county.
2. Maddy treasures her grandfather's diary because it (chronicles, chronic) his journey to America and his first years in this country.
3. My parents always turn down the (thermostat, thermometer) at night.
4. Ms. Chaudhry's class is going to the (phonograph, symphony) on Thursday, and they will get to meet the conductor after the performance.

NAME ______________________

Lesson 4.5 Greek Roots

meter = measure	(milli**meter**)	**micro** = small	(**micro**chip)
graph = write	(photo**graph**)	**ast** = star	(**ast**ronomy)
scope = see	(stetho**scope**)	**ology** = the study of	(ge**ology**)

Read the sentences below. Underline the Greek root from the pair in parentheses that will correctly complete the bold word.

1. The distance to Toronto was written in **kilo______s** on the highway sign, so it took us a minute to convert it into miles. (scope, meter)
2. When we finally arrived at the hotel, we were hungry, so we made some popcorn in the ______**wave** oven in our room. (ast, micro)
3. I was excited to find out that Riley Shaw, who plays a **crimin______** expert on TV, was staying in our hotel. (ology, graph)
4. He **auto______ed** a photo for me, and my mom snapped a few pictures of us together. (graph, meter)
5. Dad always wanted to be an ______**ronomer**, so tomorrow we're going to visit the Ontario Science Centre. (micro, ast)
6. Everyone wanted to visit the CN Tower, Toronto's famous landmark, and my little brother bought a **kaleido______** in the gift shop. (meter, scope)

Complete each sentence below. If you need help, you may use a dictionary.

1. *Musicology* is ______________________________________.
2. *Psychology* is ______________________________________.
3. *Volcanology* is ______________________________________.
4. *Zoology* is ______________________________________.
5. *Mythology* is ______________________________________.

NAME ______________________

Lesson 4.6 Latin Roots

Like Greek roots, **Latin roots** can help you determine the meanings of unfamiliar words.

aud = hear	(**aud**ible)	**ann, enn** = year	(**ann**iversary)
vid, vis = see	(**vid**eo)	**liber** = free	(**liber**ate)
mar = sea	(sub**mar**ine)	**aqua** = water	(**aqua**tic)
ped = foot	(**ped**estal)		

Circle the word that matches each definition below.

1. occurring once a year

biennial   annual   aquatic

2. a large room where people go to hear or see a performance

auditorium   audience   revision

3. freedom

liberal   liberty   impede

4. an insect that has many pairs of legs

pedestrian   aqueduct   millipede

5. a color of bluish-green that looks like water

aquamarine   marine   mariner

6. nautical; of or relating to the sea

submarine   liberate   maritime

7. the part of a bicycle that is operated by the foot

pedestal   pedal   peddler

Phonics Connection

Find three words in the activity above in which **y** makes different sounds, and write them on the lines.

______________   ______________   ______________

NAME ________________

Lesson 4.6 Latin Roots

port = carry	(trans**port**)	**struct** = build	(**struct**ure)
rupt = break	(ab**rupt**)	**tract** = pull or drag	(at**tract**)
scrib, script = write	(in**scrib**e)	**claim, clam** = shout; cry out	(pro**claim**)

Complete each sentence with a word from the box and circle the Latin roots.

subtract	interrupting	subscribes	transportation	exclaimed

1. The Getty family ________________ to four magazines and two newspapers.
2. "My soccer team made it to the championship!" ________________ Tyler.
3. It's hard for Leah to talk on the phone because her twin brothers are always ________________.
4. Remember to ________________ your expenses from your profits when you calculate the figures from the yard sale.
5. For his report on the history of ________________, Luis researched cars, trains, airplanes, and boats.

Read each word below. On the first line, define the word. On the second line, write a sentence using it. You may use a dictionary if you need help.

1. structure ________________________________

   ____
2. erupt ________________________________

   ____
3. prescribe ________________________________

   ____
4. portable ________________________________

   ____

NAME ______________________

Review Greek and Latin Roots

Use the table to help you remember the meanings of the roots you learned.

Latin		Greek	
aud = hear	**aqua** = water	**chron** = time	**meter** = measure
vid, vis = see	**port** = carry	**bio** = life	**graph** = write
mar = sea	**rupt** = break	**cycl** = circle, ring	**scope** = see
ped = foot	**scrib, script** = write	**micro** = small	**man** = hand
liber = free	**struct** = build	**phon** = sound	**ast** = star
tract = pull	**ann, enn** = year	**ology** = the study of	**therm** = heat
claim, clam = shout; cry out			

Read the sentences below. Underline the word from the pair in parentheses that correctly completes each sentence. If the word you chose contains a Greek root, write **G** on the line. If it contains a Latin root, write **L**.

1. ______ After they went ice skating at Billings Pond, Jordan and Eliza drank the hot chocolate from a (thermos, thermal).

2. ______ How are you planning to (subscribe, construct) a working volcano for the science fair?

3. ______ The (sociologist, porter) carried the Herreras' luggage from their car to their room in the hotel.

4. ______ Mackenzie just finished reading a (biography, autograph) of golfer Michelle Wie, and now she wants to take golf lessons.

5. ______ The results of the (chronicle, audition) will be posted on the bulletin board after school on Tuesday.

6. ______ Ms. Whitman said that we should organize the events in (manual, chronological) order.

7. ______ The words *assistance* and *assistants* are (homophones, autographs).

NAME ____________________

Review Greek and Latin Roots

Read the clues below. Choose the word from the box that matches each clue and write the answer in the numbered space in the crossword puzzle.

transport	aqueduct	exclaim	chronicle	pedestrian	cyclone
disrupt	astronaut	microchip	attract	anniversary	

Across

1. a pipe that transports water
3. to interrupt or stop the progress of
4. a storm in which the wind blows in rings
6. to say loudly or forcefully
8. a person traveling by foot
9. the day each year marking a special event
10. to carry or move

Down

1. to pull or draw together
2. a very small piece of electronic equipment
5. an account of events in the order in which they happened
7. a person who travels into space

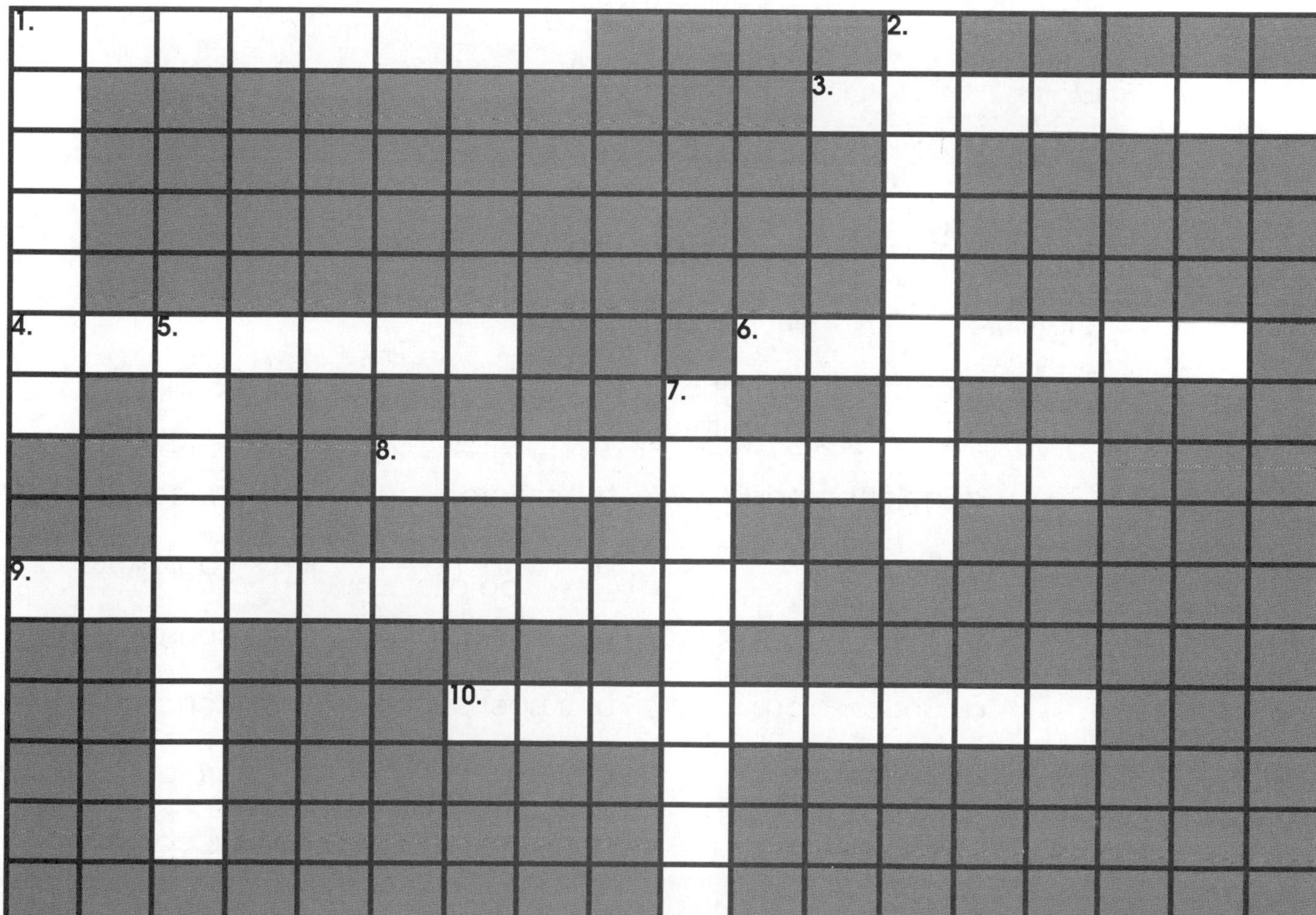

NAME ______________________

Lesson 4.7 Pronunciation Key and Respellings

Respellings, or **phonetic spellings**, are found beside entry words in a dictionary and show how the words should be pronounced. A **pronunciation key** is a guide to using the letters and symbols found in respellings. A pronunciation key is usually located on every other page in a dictionary.

Use the pronunciation key below to answer the questions in this lesson.

PRONUNCIATION KEY

/a/ = **a**t, t**a**p	/u/ = **u**p, c**u**t	/ə/ = a (**a**round, **a**bout)
/ā/ = **a**pe, s**ay**	/ū/ = **u**se, c**u**te	e (bett**e**r, tak**e**n)
/ä/ = f**a**r, h**ea**rt	/ü/ = r**u**le, c**oo**l	i (rabb**i**t, penc**i**l)
/â/ = c**a**re, h**ai**r	/u̇/ = p**u**ll, b**oo**k	o (doct**o**r, lem**o**n)
	/û/ = t**u**rn, v**e**rb	u (**u**pon, circ**u**s)
/e/ = **e**nd, g**e**t		
/ē/ = **e**ven, m**e**	/ch/ = **ch**in, tea**ch**	
/ê/ = p**i**erce, f**ea**r		
	/ng/ = si**ng**, ha**ng**	
/i/ = **i**t, f**i**t		
/ī/ = **i**ce, t**ie**	/sh/ = **sh**op, ru**sh**	
/o/ = h**o**t, f**a**ther	/th/ = **th**in, bo**th**	
/ō/ = **o**ld, s**o**	/t͟h/ = **th**is, smoo**th**	
/ô/ = s**o**ng, b**ough**t		
/ȯ/ = f**o**rk, c**o**rn	/hw/ = **wh**ite, **wh**y	
/oi/ = **oi**l, b**oy**		
/ou/ = **ou**t, h**ou**se	/zh/ = trea**su**re, bei**ge**	

On the line, write the letter of the word that contains the sound shown. Use the pronunciation key above as a guide to the sounds.

1. _____ /ō/ **a.** neighborhood **b.** mistletoe **c.** random
2. _____ /ä/ **a.** heartless **b.** mustache **c.** fragrant
3. _____ /ē/ **a.** inventory **b.** yearning **c.** conservation
4. _____ /zh/ **a.** unconscious **b.** suspension **c.** conclusion
5. _____ /u/ **a.** enthusiastic **b.** shove **c.** profound
6. _____ /ə/ **a.** rosebush **b.** sheep **c.** accomplish
7. _____ /ô/ **a.** fraud **b.** clothing **c.** mispronounce

NAME ______________________________

Lesson 4.7 Pronunciation Key and Respellings

Read the following musical definitions. Some of the words have been spelled phonetically. On the line, rewrite each bold word in its common form.

The world is filled with **di' frənt** __________________ musical **stīlz** __________________.

Most likely you've **hûrd** __________________ of rock and roll, country, hip-hop, and jazz, but what about these other genres?

AFROBEAT—This West African style of music **kəm bīnz'** __________________ the instruments and **mel' ə dēz** __________________ of local **fōk** __________________ music with American soul and R&B.

FLAMENCO—The **trə dish' ə nəl** __________________ music of the Roma people of Spain. It has **rith' mic** __________________ clapping and foot stomping that **ə kum' pə nēz** __________________ highly emotional singing and **gi tär'** __________________ playing.

RAGA—The droning melody heard in Indian **klas' i kəl** __________________ music and **ū' zhü ə lē** __________________ played on the sitar—an **in' strə mənt** __________________ similar to the guitar that can have as many as 20 strings.

SAMBA—An **up' bēt'** __________________ style of Brazilian music that grew out of **ri lij' əs** __________________ songs and dances **brôt** __________________ to the **rē' jən** __________________ by African slaves.

SON—Cuban music that blends Spanish-style guitar, South African **pər cush' ən** __________________ instruments, and rousing horns into a danceable mixture.

QAWWALI—An Islamic musical style that is hundreds of **yêrz** __________________ old. These songs, which last about half an hour, usually begin **kwī' it lē** __________________ before building to a fast, hypnotic rhythm.

NAME ______________________________

Lesson 4.7 Pronunciation Key and Respellings

Read the recipe below. Underline the words that the respellings in the box stand for. You do not need to underline the same word twice.

/sī' dər/ /ku̇k' ē/ /stȯrd/ /jüs/ /i vap' ə rāts'/
/so' fənd/ /ap' əl sôs'/ /sin' ə mən/ /red' ē/ /jin' jər/ /leth' ər/
/uv' ən/ /in krēs'/ /pē' səz/ /prô' ses' ər/ /früt/

Fruit Leather

Ingredients: 5 apples, $\frac{1}{2}$ cup apple cider or apple juice, $\frac{1}{2}$ teaspoon cinnamon, $\frac{1}{4}$ teaspoon nutmeg, $\frac{1}{4}$ teaspoon ground ginger

You'll also need: a knife, a blender or food processor, a pot with a lid, a slotted spoon, a wooden spoon, a cookie sheet, and wax paper

- Peel and core the apples, and then slice them into pieces. Place them in the pot with the cider or juice, cover, and simmer over medium heat until the apples have softened. If all the moisture evaporates, add a bit more juice.
- Allow the mixture to cool for a few minutes. Use the slotted spoon to carefully remove the chunks of fruit. Blend the apples until they form a sauce about the same thickness as applesauce. Add the spices and stir until blended.
- Line the cookie sheet with wax paper. Spoon the applesauce onto the sheet, and spread it around at a thickness of about $\frac{1}{4}$ inch.
- Heat the oven to 140°. Place the cookie sheet in the oven, and leave the door cracked a few inches. In four to six hours, your fruit leather will be done. You can be sure it's ready when it feels barely sticky to the touch and it peels back easily from the wax paper.
- Cut the fruit leather into strips, and wrap it in plastic wrap, or simply roll it up with the wax paper. When stored at room temperature, it lasts about a month. You can also refrigerate or freeze it to increase its life span.

* Remember, you should always ask an adult for help in the kitchen when using knives or the stove.

NAME ______________________________

Lesson 4.7 Pronunciation Key and Respellings

Read the sentences below. Rewrite each bold word using the letters and symbols in the pronunciation key. You do not need to place the accents, or stress marks. If you need help, you may use a dictionary, but remember that not all pronunciation keys are exactly the same.

1. Alvin Ailey, born in Rogers, Texas, in 1931, always had an **interest** ____________________ in and a **talent** ____________________ for the arts.
2. Ailey began his dance **training** ____________________ with two very well-known **professionals** ____________________—Katherine Dunham and Lester Horton.
3. Mr. Horton founded the first **racially** ____________________ integrated dance company in the United States, and when he died in 1953, Ailey became the new **director** ____________________.
4. The Civil Rights Movement was beginning to **make** ____________________ its way **through** ____________________ the country, and Ailey supported it by celebrating African-American **culture** ____________________ through dance.
5. In 1958, Ailey opened his own dance **company** ____________________ in New York, called the Alvin Ailey **American** ____________________ Dance Theater.
6. For Ailey, dance was a way to express himself and **communicate** ____________________ with the world about **race** ____________________, power, beauty, art, and life.
7. Today, Ailey's name and work remain **among** ____________________ the most recognizable in the **world** ____________________ of dance.

Phonics Connection

On the lines, write two bold words from above in which the /sh/ sound is not spelled **sh**.

____________________ ____________________

NAME ______________________________

Lesson 4.8 Accent Marks

An accent mark (′) tells which syllable of a word is stressed, or said with more force. Try saying /ə kad′ ə mē/ with the stress on different syllables. Can you hear the difference when the correct syllable is stressed?

- Some words have two accents. The **primary** accent is usually bold. The syllable with the **secondary** accent is said with less force.

  /ûrth′ kwāk′/ /pôl′ ē wôg′/ /ek′ sər sīz′/
- Remember, the schwa does not appear in stressed syllables.

Read each bold word out loud. Circle the letter of the respelling in which the primary accent mark is placed correctly.

1. multiplied	**a.** mul′ tə plīd′	**b.** mul′ tə plīd′
2. jury	**a.** jûr′ ē	**b.** jûr ē′
3. songbird	**a.** sông′ bûrd′	**b.** sông′ bûrd′
4. window	**a.** win′ dō	**b.** win dō′
5. carpenter	**a.** kär pən′ tər	**b.** kär′ pən tər

Read the sentences below. Add the primary accent to each bold respelling.

1. One of the best things you can do to help the /**en vī rən mənt**/ is to reduce, reuse, and /**rē sī kəl**/.
2. Make your /**pā pər**/ last twice as long by printing on the back of each page.
3. /**in sted**/ of buying /**bôt ld**/ water in plastic bottles, bring your own /**rē ūz ə bəl**/ water jug with you /**hwâr ev ər**/ you go.
4. /**dō nāt**/ clothes you've outgrown to /**châr i tēz**/, or cut them into rags that can be used in place of paper /**tou əlz**/.
5. Read /**lā bəlz**/, and use products made from recycled /**mə têr ē əlz**/.
6. If you /**viz it**/ someplace that doesn't recycle, write a letter telling the /**kum pə nē**/ it's important to you and /**ik splān ing**/ how they can get started.

NAME ____________________

Lesson 4.8 Accent Marks

All the words listed below contain both a primary and a secondary accent. Circle the primary accent in each word.

1. /ə kôm′ ə dā′ shənz/
2. /hel′ i kôp′ tər/
3. /rat′l snāk′/
4. /lō′ kə mō′ shən/
5. /wôl′ nut′/
6. /sum′ bôd′ ē/
7. /gâr′ ən tē′/
8. /pär tis′ ə pāt′/

Some multiple-meaning words are spelled the same but pronounced differently. For example, *project* can be pronounced /prə jekt′/ or /prôj′ ekt′/. The meaning is different depending on which syllable is stressed.

Each bold word below has two possible pronunciations. Beside each phonetic spelling, write the letter of the matching definition.

1. **contract** kôn′ tract′ _____ kən tract′ _____
   a. to shrink; to become infected with **b.** a verbal or written agreement
2. **minute** min′ it _____ mī nüt′ _____
   a. a unit of time **b.** small or tiny
3. **object** ôb′ jikt _____ ôb′ jekt′ _____
   a. a noun or pronoun **b.** to disagree or oppose
4. **refuse** ri fūz′ _____ ref′ ūz _____
   a. garbage or trash **b.** to decline or be unwilling
5. **compress** kəm pres′ _____ kôm′ pres′ _____
   a. a soft bandage **b.** squash or press together
6. **upset** up set′ _____ up′ set′ _____
   a. to tip over or capsize **b.** when the favored team loses
7. **conduct** kən dukt′ _____ kôn′ dukt _____
   a. how a person acts **b.** to lead, especially an orchestra

NAME ______________________

Review Respellings and Accent Marks

Look at each picture below. On the line, write the respelling of the word that names the picture. Include the primary accent mark in each respelling.

______________ ______________ ______________

______________ ______________ ______________

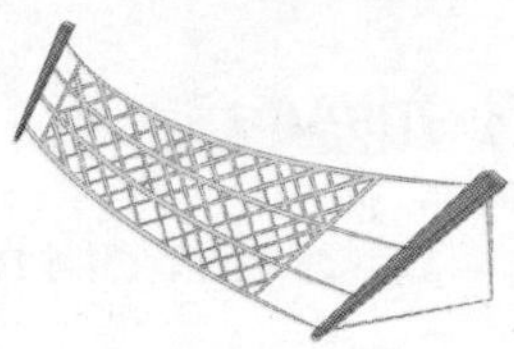

______________ ______________ ______________

Read the newspaper headlines below. Underline the word from the pair in parentheses in which the accent or accents are correctly placed.

1. Local Teen Wins (rē jə′ nəl, rē′ jə nəl) Spelling Championship
2. (hev ē′, hev′ ē) Weekend Storms Knock Out Power to 150,000 Residents
3. Clausen Withdraws from Race Three Weeks Before (i lek′ shən, i lek shən′)
4. Plans for New East Side Shopping Mall—Why Are (pē pəl′, pē′ pəl) Protesting?
5. (mi stêr′ ē əs, mi′ stêr ē əs) Briefcase Found Containing $2,000
6. (lō′ kəl, lō kəl′) Funding Cuts Mean Arts School May Have to Shut Its Doors
7. (ə non′ ə məs, ə non ə məs′) Donor Contributes $45,000 to Renovation of Kaufmann Theater
8. Hollywood Comes to Town for Filming of New (ak shən′, ak′ shən) Flick

NAME ____________________

Review Respellings and Accent Marks

Read the sentences below. Underline the stressed syllable in the bold word. On the line, write the word that matches each bold respelling.

1. Chislehurst Caves, located in a suburb of London, are **/ak chü ə lē/** ____________________ former chalk and flint mines.
2. No one is sure exactly how old the caves are, but the **/ûr lē ist/** ____________________ known **/ref ər əns/** ____________________ to them is A.D. 1250.
3. The caves **/in klüd/** ____________________ approximately 22 miles of **/tun əlz/** ____________________ and passageways.
4. The depth of the caves **/vär ēz/** ____________________ from 40 feet below the **/sûr fəs/** ____________________ to about 150 feet underground.
5. The temperature of the caves remains **/sted ē/** ____________________, summer or winter, at 45 **/di grēz/** ____________________ Fahrenheit.
6. The last time the caves were used as mines was in the 1830s, but they have had many **/u<u>th</u> ər/** ____________________ uses since that time.
7. Mushrooms grow well in dark, damp **/plā sez/** ____________________, so for some time the caves were used as a sort of mushroom farm.
8. During World War II, the caves were turned into an **/ə māz ing/** ____________________ underground **/sit ē/** ____________________.
9. They were a **/kən vēn yənt/** ____________________ air raid shelter for Londoners.
10. The caves were wired for **/i lek tris i tē/** ____________________ and contained a **/hôs pi tl/** ____________________, chapel, movie theater, and gym.
11. During the war, the caves were filled with about 15,000 people seeking shelter **/ev rē/** ____________________ night.

REVIEW: CHAPTER 4 LESSONS 7–8

Answer Key

page 6

1. began
2. because
3. legend
4. segment
5. electric

1. HC, SC
2. SG, HG
3. SC, HC
4. HC, HG
5. SC, HC, HG
6. SG
7. SC

page 7

<u>**Hard g**</u>	<u>**Hard c**</u>
geyser	directly
agree	including
gurgle	located
underground	occur
magma	rock
longer	cooler
begins	continues
again	cools
gallons	back
	cycle
	predictable
	spectacle

<u>**Soft g**</u>	<u>**Soft c**</u>
regions	Iceland
largest	cycle
passages	distance
giant	

page 8

1. a, d
2. b, c
3. c, d
4. b, c
5. a, d
6. b, d
7. b, c
8. a, c

<u>/s/ sound</u>	<u>/z/ sound</u>
basketball	preservative
restless	refusal
frustrate	composition
postpone	newspaper

<u>/zh/ sound</u>	<u>/sh/ sound</u>
precision	permission
casually	expansion
visionary	sugar
division	tissue

page 9

/s/, /s/, /s/, /z/, /s/, /z/, /z/, /zh/, /z/, /s/, /z/, /zh/, /sh/, /z/, /s/, /sh/, /s/, /z/, /zh/, /zh/

page 10

because
refrigerator
Antarctica
centipede
frogs
Cinderella

1. soft **g**
2. hard **g**
3. soft **g**
4. hard **c**
5. soft **c**
6. hard **c**

page 11

1. unusual
2. clothes
3. insurance
4. positive
5. teaspoon

page 12

1. /ch/, /k/
2. /sh/

Dear Diary,

My grandparents gave me a season pass to the art museum for a birthday present this year. It's only four subway stops away from our new apartment, so I can visit as frequently as I like. I've been there several times on field trips, but it is so large, that I think it would take a whole lifetime to know every piece of art. The new expansion will be complete this spring, and I can't wait to see what has changed.

When Isabel and I go this weekend, I'd like to spend some time looking at the work of the Impressionists. In Mr. Yang's class, we recently learned about the issue that a group of artists had in France during the late 1800s. The French Academy was powerful, and they pressured artists to create certain types of work. The group that would later become known as the Impressionists had their own vision of what art could be. Maybe someday I'll have the pleasure of seeing my own artwork hanging proudly on those same walls.

3. /sh/, /ch/, /sh/
4. /sh/, /ch/, /ch/
5. /sh/, /sh/, /sh/
6. /sh/
7. /k/
8. /ch/
9. /ch/, /sh/, /k/

page 13

1. theater
2. northern
3. Philippines
4. wholesome
5. sympathy
6. whimper
7. pharmacy

y	e	h	a	n	o	r	t	h	e	r	n	v	e
t	p	h	i	l	i	p	p	i	n	e	s	n	m
o	h	n	t	c	a	s	x	w	b	t	n	n	o
g	a	y	r	e	b	e	w	h	u	a	p	m	s
f	r	r	y	o	a	x	e	l	w	e	n	b	e
y	m	f	g	d	l	l	o	m	b	h	z	j	l
h	a	f	e	w	s	y	m	p	a	t	h	y	o
o	c	l	h	y	r	e	q	e	v	c	d	s	h
k	y	t	u	n	c	w	e	r	b	q	a	k	w

Answer Key

page 14

1. Hockey is a team sport played on ice by players wearing skates.
2. It is not really surprising that hockey is most popular in regions of the world that stay relatively cold, such as Canada, Finland, and Russia.
3. Because a rubber disc called a puck can fly at speeds of more than 100 miles per hour, hockey can be a rough and dangerous game.
4. Even plenty of protective equipment isn't always enough to keep a player safe.
5. A goaltender's job is to keep the puck from entering the net and thus keep the opposing team from scoring a point.
6. The goalie may block a shot with his or her body, which is well padded with protective gear, or he or she may use a hockey stick as the rest of the players do.
7. Most ice hockey teams are comprised of men, but women have played the game since at least the 1800s. Today, the number of women playing the sport is rapidly increasing.

page 15

ch, th, sh, ng, ch, sh, ch, Th, ng, ch, th, ng, ng, sh, th, th, th, ch, ng, ch, ch

page 16

1. The secret to Aunt Lulu's meatloaf is using breadcrumbs made from homemade sourdough bread.
2. The hiker filled her knapsack with food, water, and a map.
3. Primates are similar to humans in their use of the opposable thumb.
4. The Hahns decided to take the scenic route through the mountains, even though it added a couple of hours to their trip.
5. Although any free man could become a knight during the Middle Ages, it was generally men from wealthy families who received this honor.
6. The plastic wrapper covering the CD was difficult to remove.

1. clumsy
2. nightmare
3. comb
4. roundtrip
5. sabotage

page 17

Vijay Mehta: When did you first know that you wanted to be a singer and songwriter?

Carson Bell: That's an interesting question. I came from a tightly knit family, and as a child, my brothers and I spent a great deal of time listening to music. We imitated what we heard, and we eventually started creating our own music.

VM: So you always knew you wanted to write music or somehow be involved in the music industry?

CB: No, it was actually a much longer road for me. I was taking the scenic way home from work one night, when I did something dumb. I had a paper cut on my thumb and I tried to look for a bandage in the glove compartment while I was driving.

VM: What happened?

CB: Well, I wrecked my car, but luckily I didn't do too much damage to myself. When I climbed out of the car, my left wrist hurt pretty badly and I had broken my kneecap but I was okay.

VM: Did the accident have an impact on your life?

CB: It absolutely did. I enjoyed my job and working in the field of science but I didn't feel the same passion for it as I had for music. I wrestled with the decision of what I really wanted to do with my life. The scenes from my childhood kept replaying themselves over and over in my mind.

VM: Is that when you went out on a limb and changed your career path?

CB: Yes, and I've never regretted my decision or felt that I had made the wrong choice. I think the knowledge of yourself and the things that are a priority to you are essential to feeling happy and fulfilled.

page 18

1. cologne
2. sigh
3. rhythm
4. switch
5. rhinoceros
6. delight
7. pledge
8. foreign
9. hatchet

1. cries	thighs	5. touch	hutch
2. claw	gnaw	6. pledge	hedge
3. richer	pitcher	7. wait	straight
4. incline	assign	8. climb	rhyme

page 19

1. dg
2. tch
3. gn
4. gh, rh
5. gn
6. Rh
7. tch
8. gn

1. b, dg
2. c, rh
3. a, gh
4. b, gn
5. a, tch
6. c, dg
7. b, gh
8. c, tch

page 20

The Mayan civilization was at its strongest between A.D. 250 and A.D. 900. It existed in what is today Guatemala, Belize, Mexico, Honduras, and El Salvador. For many years, the Mayan people were somewhat of a mystery to the historians and archaeologists who studied them. *What could have made such a powerful and advanced nation decline so drastically?* they wondered.

The Maya were proficient in agriculture and practiced the cultivation of maize (a type of corn), beans, squash, peppers, avocados, and pineapples. They had an advanced system of irrigation and also used other farming techniques, like rotating crops and building terraces.

There were more than 40 Mayan cities, and at one time, the population may have reached two million. The Maya used a system of hieroglyphic writing, similar to Egyptian hieroglyphics. The Mayan hieroglyphs, as well as inscriptions carved in rock, are important sources of information for modern-day researchers.

The Maya are considered to have been the most advanced ancient civilization in the Western Hemisphere. What caused their decline? It may have been vicious wars, natural disasters, or a disease that wiped out large portions of the population. About 800,000 people today speak Mayan languages. Many modern Maya still live an agricultural lifestyle like their ancestors did. Their preservation of the Mayan culture and traditions in modern society give it the potential to be passed along for generations to come.

page 21

1. ti
2. ci, ti
3. ti
4. ti
5. ci, ci
6. ti, ti
7. ti
8. ci
9. ci, ci
10. ci, ti
11. ti, ti
12. ti

page 22

1. c
2. a
3. a
4. b
5. c
6. b

1. lambs
2. budge
3. knew
4. wrinkled
5. hatched
6. neighed
7. designed

Answer Key

page 23

1. Possible answers: /th/: they, the /th/: thought, three, thousand, thumb, with
2. Possible answers: chopsticks, characters, chef

3–4.

Chopsticks are eating utensils used in China, Japan, Korea, and Vietnam. They are thought to have been invented in China between three and five thousand years ago and are used as tongs or pincers. They may be made of wood, bamboo, metal, bone, ivory, or even plastic. In Japan, the word *otemoto*, Japanese for *chopstick*, is often written on the wrapper in Japanese characters.

The proper way to hold chopsticks is between the thumb and fingers. The bottom stick stays stationary, while the top stick moves up and down to grasp the food. If the chef has cut the food into small pieces and the rice is sticky enough, eating with chopsticks is simple.

1. ci
2. ti
3. ti, ti

page 24

weigh; halfway; convey; everyday; veil; weekday; disobey; maintain; restrained; mermaid; swaying; reindeer; hey

page 25

May; today; stayed; Eight; remain; essays; convey; Hooray; praise; neighbor; details; obtain; subway; survey; Friday; pay

page 26

1. ee
2. ea
3. ie
4. ey
5. ea; ee
6. ea
7. ea

1. Chimpanzees; monkeys; comedies
2. Field; Dreams; movie
3. Chief; nominee; Haley
4. Eddie; donkey
5. lead; Dixie
6. Cheaper; dreams

page 27

1. ordeal
2. attorney
3. heartbeat
4. antifreeze
5. bittersweet
6. Tennessee
7. kidney
8. parsley
9. cleave

page 28

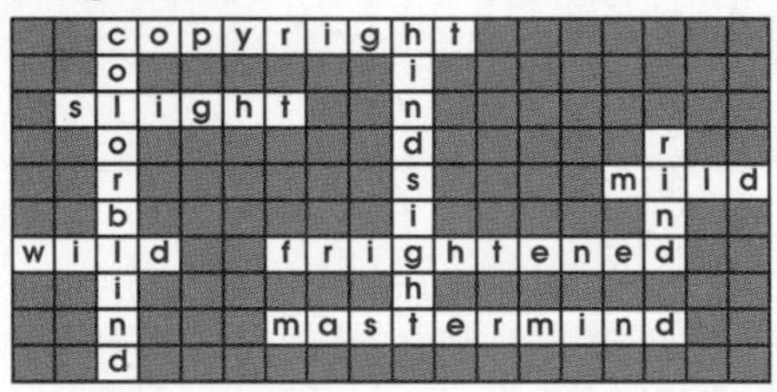

page 29

1. b, d
2. a, b, c
3. a, d
4. b
5. a, c

igh	**ind**
might	reminders
nighttime	find
moonlight	
plight	**ild**
insight	wild
delightful	child's
stoplight	

page 30

1. mold
2. outgrow
3. toll
4. most
5. charcoal
6. blindfold
7. scarecrow
8. scold
9. host
10. boast
11. scroll
12. glow
13. crossroads
14. stroll
15. billfold
16. croak
17. almost

page 31

ow, oa, oa, oa, oa, ow, old, old, oa, oll, ow, ow, old, ow, old, ow, old, ow, ow, ow, ow

page 32

ee; ee
ea
ey
igh
ea; ild
ey
ow; ee
oa; ay
ea; ow; ai
ea
ea; ea
old; oa; ea
oll

page 33

1. sustain, convey
2. uptight, unwinding
3. roaming, withhold
4. oversleep, attorney
5. enrolled, sugarcoat

Answer Key

6. decay, reins

1. long **e**, long **i**
2. long **o**, long **o**, long **a**
3. long **e**
4. long **o**/long **o**, long **e**
5. long **a**, long **o**, long **e**, long **a**
6. long **e**, long **o**

page 34

1. b the act of chasing something in order to catch it
2. e occurring later than planned or scheduled
3. f not wearing shoes
4. a an annoyance
5. c the means by which a person earns a living
6. d a small, cozy, or hidden area

a. nuisance
b. pursuit
c. livelihood
d. nook
e. overdue
f. barefoot

1. papoose
2. booth
3. could; curlicue
4. revenue
5. cruising

page 35

oo, oo, ew, ew, oo, oo, oo, ue, ue, ou, ui, ui, ou, ue, ui, oo

page 36

1. Although; audience; all
2. author
3. awful
4. because; caution
5. drawn
6. Beanstalk
7. granddaughter; caught
8. smaller; brawnier
9. taught

page 37

1. chalkboard
2. basketball
3. scrawled
4. asphalt
5. crosswalk

6. installed

1. aw
2. all
3. au
4. alk
5. au
6. aw

page 38

1. I am a company or person for whom others work. Some might call me the boss. employer
2. I am a verb that means to *lift* or *pull up*. You could use me in this sentence: *The girls helped their dad ____ the sails.* hoist
3. The word *faithfulness* is a synonym for me. I describe a quality that good friends or family members show for one another. loyalty
4. Founded in 1843, I am Iowa's capital city. Des Moines
5. I am a feeling of great happiness or pleasure. joyfulness
6. I am another word for *bother* or *irritate*. annoy
7. I am a person's perspective or the way he or she sees things. viewpoint

1. toil
2. convoy
3. moisture
4. spoiled

page 39

What kinds of things do you read on the computer? Have you ever tried reading an e-book, or electronic book? What about a newspaper article or your favorite magazine? For many people, it's difficult to spend long amounts of time in front of a computer screen. They would rather find a more comfortable place in the house to read, like a cozy chair or the couch. A laptop computer is portable, but it is still bulkier than a magazine or small book. It's also hard for someone reading in a car or outdoors to see the screen in bright light.

Several renowned companies on the cutting edge of technology are now working on some ideas that would forever change the way people read. How does the idea of electronic paper sound to you? It's difficult to explain exactly how this concept works. The basic idea, though, is that the battery-powered paper is filled with tiny capsules. Each capsule contains black and white particles that carry an electric charge. Using the electricity in each capsule, a computer program determines whether the black or white particles are allowed to come to the surface of the paper. The black particles form patterns that create letters, symbols, and words. When you "turn the page," different particles rise to the surface and form the words and pictures on the next page of the book or magazine.

Although it seems like something that might be found in a science fiction novel, it's possible that in the future a single piece of electronic paper could somehow hold the contents of an entire book. The countdown to the books of the future has begun.

page 40

1. compound
2. rejoice
3. whirlpool
4. suitable
5. awkward
6. shook
7. scowl
8. squall

9. oyster
10. true

f	a	h	m	s	d	g	i	o	e	b	c	a	a
j	w	j	r	t	q	l	l	a	u	q	s	b	n
w	k	h	v	c	r	w	u	l	l	v	u	f	r
n	w	x	l	c	e	o	t	y	h	s	l	s	u
r	a	b	d	r	h	c	a	i	m	k	t	f	z
e	r	k	r	q	l	s	o	o	v	d	a	h	r
j	d	h	j	b	s	p	l	k	c	z	b	p	e
o	m	m	r	w	h	n	o	g	l	l	l	d	t
l	e	d	n	u	o	p	m	o	c	f	e	n	s
c	h	j	m	a	o	c	t	u	l	s	w	b	y
e	n	m	p	l	k	r	e	t	r	u	e	q	o

page 41

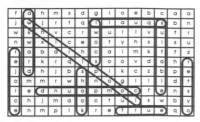

au; ow; aw; all; ow; ue; oo; ow; oy; au; oi; ow; ue; all; oi; ew; oy; ow; ew; all; ow; ow; au

page 42

1. limber
2. cardinal
3. scallop
4. passion
5. diary

1. regənəl
2. ərome
3. mountəneer
4. florəl
5. ancestərs
6. koalə
7. pyrəmids

page 43

Throughout history, our **nation** and its **citizens** have had to endure a number of difficult and trying **moments**. Few events were as sad as the **assassinations** of presidents Abraham Lincoln and John F. Kennedy. Although they are not discussed as **often**, the deaths of James Garfield and William McKinley were equally shocking to the **Americans** of their time.

President James Garfield took office on March 4, 1881. Only four months **later**, on July 2, Garfield was walking through a Washington, D.C., railroad station when Charles J. Guiteau shot him. Garfield lived for **another** 80 days, but **medical** knowledge during that time was limited. On **September** 19, President Garfield passed **away**. He had been president for only six and a half months.

President William McKinley began his **second** term in March 1901. Due to America's **victory** in the Spanish-American War, McKinley had **easily** defeated William Jennings Bryan in the **previous** fall's election. In September 1901, McKinley **traveled** to Buffalo, New York, to give a speech at the Pan-American **Exposition**. It was at this World's Fair that tragedy would strike.

On September 6, McKinley stood at the front of a line of people waiting to shake the president's hand. Slowly, Leon Czolgosz made his way through the line. Czolgosz was an **anarchist**—someone who believes that all forms of government are bad and should be **abolished**. Although many anarchists were **peaceful**, others **performed violent** acts.

When Czolgosz reached the front of the line, he shot McKinley and was immediately **taken** into custody. McKinley was rushed to the **hospital** in an **ambulance**, making him the first president to ride in an **automobile**. Sadly, McKinley died of his wounds eight days later.

Answer Key

page 44
1. tropical
2. mammals
3. Environmental
4. Local, animals
5. materials, travel
6. people, jungle
7. petals
8. resembles
9. muscles, tackle

page 45
1. custom
2. ceramics
3. postal
4. astronaut
5. husband

1. In 1910, Robert Baden-Powell founded the Girl Guides of Great Britain as a **coun·ter·part** to the group for boys he began in 1908.
2. In 1912, Juliette Low started the Girl Scouts, a **sim·i·lar** organization in the United States.
3. The Girl Scouts and Girl Guides both **fo·cus** on leadership, **char·ac·ter**, community, outdoor activities, and service.
4. In **A·mer·i·ca** the five age groups are called the *Daisies, Brownies, Juniors,* ***Ca·dettes****,* and *Seniors.*
5. Today, there are nearly 10 **mil·lion** members in 144 countries.

page 46
1. policy
2. yonder
3. rhythm
4. pastry
5. firefly
6. enemy
7. myself
8. mythical

page 47
1. long **e**, long **e**, long **i**, **y**
2. **y**, long **i**
3. long **e**, long **e**, **y**
4. long **i**, long **e**, short **i**/long **e**
5. long **e**, long **e**

1. anchovy	icy
2. physician	Olympian
3. spying	magnify
4. years	yucca
5. backyard	yield
6. everything	financially
7. hyena	dying
8. yonder	canyon

page 48
Alvarez'
Scarf; Girl
Monster; Walter; Myers
North
Birmingham; Christopher; Curtis
Charlotte
Summer; German; Soldier
Morning; Girl; Dorris
Iceberg; Hermit; Arthur
Virginia
Sports
Piranhas
Borning
Garden; Burnett
Survival; Gordon; Korman

ar: Answers will vary.
er: Answers will vary.
ur: Answers will vary.

page 49
smirk; seashore; swerve; mirth; midterm; sunburn; bizarre; lifeguard; lurking; emerge; bookmark; purse; carnivore; adverb; suburb; splurge; affordable; postmark; quirky; thirst; discord; proverb; whirl

page 50

1. a person who offers to do something, often for free	volunteer
2. a list of questions used for gathering information	questionnaire
3. to guide a vehicle using a wheel	steer
4. not common; something that doesn't occur often	rare
5. to spread a sticky or greasy material	smear
6. a game of cards one plays alone	solitaire
7. equipment	gear
8. to be cautious of something	beware

1. are
2. air
3. air
4. eer
5. are, ear, are

page 51
1. disappear
2. millionaire
3. solitaire
4. career
5. wearable
6. auctioneer
7. smeared
8. bear

1. fairly
2. nearly
3. peer
4. threadbare
5. dearest

page 52

Too many **an·i·mals** in the world don't have a place to call home or **peo·ple** to protect them. **Thou·sands** of these animals get a **sec·ond** chance at a **spe·cial** place called Best Friends Animal Sanctuary, located in Kanab, Utah. The motto of Best Friends is "No more homeless pets."

Today, more than 1,500 animals live at the sanctuary. There are plenty of **com·mon** house pets, like cats and dogs, but Best Friends is also home to horses, pigs, goats, owls, rabbits, and **doz·ens** of other **va·ri·e·ties** of critters. Some are sick, and many were **a·ban·doned** or **a·bused**. Best Friends **wel·comes** all animals, regardless of their history. Once an animal enters the sanctuary, it will be treated with kindness and respect. Hundreds of animals find good homes through the **ef·forts** of Best Friends. The animals that don't find new families are still guaranteed a safe and happy place to live forever.

Best Friends works with groups all **a·round** the country to make the lives of animals better. They educate people about the importance of spaying and neutering pets. They also have the best interests of animals in mind when a crisis **oc·curs**. There's no doubt that the furry and feathered **crea·tures** of the world are lucky to have the folks at Best Friends looking out for them.

On the line, write the sound **y** makes in each bold word (long **i**, short **i**, **y**, or long **e**). Circle the word beside it that contains the same sound.

1. short **i**; rhythm
2. long **i**; magnify
3. **y**; yowl
4. long **e**; stingy

5. short **i**; physics

page 53
carpet: particular, start, Karla
turning: together, first, similar, wander, concerned, swirl, burst, Silverstein, familiar
orchid: forms, short, important, sorts, brainstorming
fairly: sharing, carefully
clear: career, Shakespeare

page 54

Base Word	Add **ed**	Add **ing**
cherish	**cherished**	cherishing
struggle	**struggled**	**struggling**
format	formatted	**formatting**
scribble	**scribbled**	**scribbling**
enforce	**enforced**	**enforcing**
identify	identified	**identifying**
untie	untied	**untying**

1. demonstrate
2. accompany
3. create

identify, identifying, untying

page 55
means; fit; produces; uses; switch; save; burn; purchase; teaches; wishes; encourages; passes; means; save; exchange

page 56

Base Word	Add **er**	Add **est**
shiny	**shinier**	**sniniest**
rare	rarer	**rarest**
red	**redder**	reddest
angry	**angrier**	**angriest**
light	**lighter**	lightest
lovely	**lovelier**	loveliest
free	**freer**	**freest**
shallow	shallower	**shallowest**
slim	**slimmer**	**slimmest**
strange	**stranger**	**strangest**
rough	**rougher**	roughest
sleepy	sleepier	**sleepiest**

page 57
most excited, squeakier, most frustrating, more smoothly, most interesting, earlier, most popular, safer

page 58
playing, inspired, hired, named, measured, completed, sewing, finished, flying, tried, defending, waved, announced

page 59
Danny: easier, funniest, latest
Austin: kinder, gentler, most compassionate, toughest, smartest, most original, brighter
Christina: younger, most trustworthy, healthier, more interesting, bigger

drip relax polish
occupy drag empty

page 60
trees, bushes, houses, poles, stories, countries, leaves, blooms, masses, vines, conditions, branches, bridges, roofs, enemies, lives

page 61
1. tomato
2. kangaroo
3. pistachio
4. burrito
5. flamingo
6. solo
7. pueblo

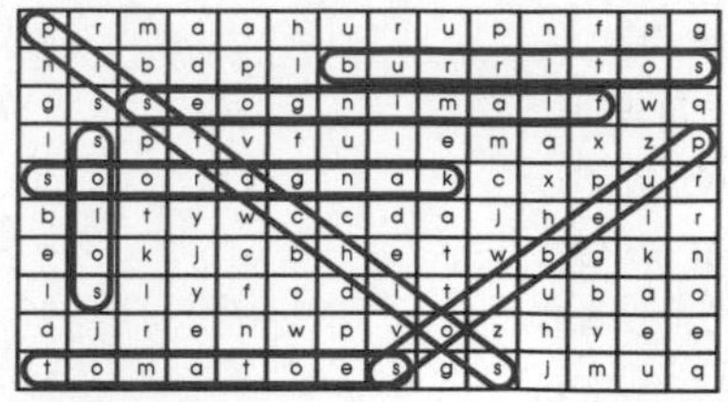

page 62
1. children
2. trout
3. feet
4. oasis
5. species
6. teeth
7. mouse
8. deer
9. goose's

page 63
1. Answers will vary but should include the word *teeth*.
2. Answers will vary but should include the word *traffic*.
3. Answers will vary but should include the word *women*.
4. Answers will vary but should include the word *fish*.
5. Answers will vary but should include the word *feet*.
6. Answers will vary but should include the word *moose*.

1. tooth, fish
2. tooth, moose's; foot

page 64
PL, PP, SP, SP, PL, SP, PL, PL, PP

Answer Key

page 65
1. Women's
2. event's
3. Angelou's
4. world's
5. Veterans'
6. Nation's
7. shuttles'

1. the drums' beat
2. the song's lyrics
3. the guitarist's solo
4. the musicians' energy
5. the keyboard's melody

page 66

Singular	Plural	Singular Possessive	Plural Possessive
colony	colonies	colony's	colonies'
waltz	waltzes	waltz's	waltzes'
coach	coaches	coach's	coaches'
banjo	banjoes	banjo's	banjoes'
city	cities	city's	cities'
portfolio	portfolios	portfolio's	portfolios'
physician	physicians	physician's	physicians'
mouse	mice	mouse's	mice's
mosquito	mosquitoes	mosquito's	mosquitoes'

1. biographies; stories
2. mysteries; novels
3. elves; ogres; folktales; legends
4. comics
5. classes
6. cookbooks; recipes; Burritos; Mangoes

page 67
1. Ladies' Reading Club
2. classes' schedules
3. mother's purse
4. children's toys
5. person's participation
6. Jake's internship
7. Trout's mouths

1. schedules, technology
2. drawing, auction

page 68
1. firewood
2. wheelchair
3. barefoot
4. rattlesnake
5. turtleneck
6. jellyfish

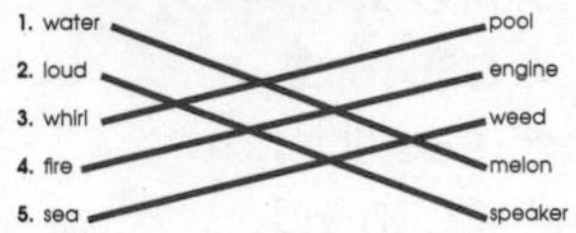

watermelon
loudspeaker
whirlpool
fire engine
seaweed

page 69
news/paper; back/yards; after/noons; week/ends; out/doors; in/side; play/ground; green/house; basket/ball; sand/box; With/out; worth/while

page 70
There're; aren't; I'd; haven't; I'm; you'd; don't; They're; won't; It's; they've; aren't; They'll; let's; might've; here's; you're; shouldn't; What're

page 71
1. have'nt; haven't
2. Im; I'm
3. instructors; instructor's
4. won't; won't
5. thats; that's
6. theres; there's
7. have'nt; haven't
8. were; we're
9. winds; wind's

1. away, stay, today, anyway
2. parachuting, assured

page 72
anybody, anyone, anything anywhere, fireplace, fireworks, firewood, firefly, firefighter, homemade, hometown, homegrown, homesick, homeroom, underground, underwater, undercover, underwear

1. corn/bread
2. ice / skate
3. tea/cup
4. foot/print
5. horse/back
6. candle/light
7. bee/hive
8. polar / bear
9. button/hole

page 73
1. you're; you are
2. you'll; you will
3. can't; can not
4. It's; it is
5. wasn't; was not
6. aren't; haven't; are not, have not
7. shouldn't; don't; should not, do not
8. There're; there are

page 74
inseparable; infrequent; immature; irrational; irresistible; impatiently; inefficient; immovable; illogical; inexperience; incapable; impolite; incorrect

page 75
1. engulf

2. encouraged
3. enrolled
4. employed
5. enlisted
6. enriched
7. envisioned
8. ensured

page 76
1. cohost; host
2. midstream; stream
3. reproduce; produce
4. rewrite; write

1. cofounded; founded together
2. rediscover; discover again
3. midsummer; middle of the summer
4. cowritten; written together
5. retold; told again
6. reassured; assured again

page 77

1. h	partly conscious	a. semisolid
2. e	connect among one another	b. nonacademic
3. l	not factual	c. semicircle
4. a	half solid	d. nonfiction
5. j	between nations	e. interconnect
6. b	not academic	f. intercoastal
7. k	partly dry	g. intercollegiate
8. d	not fiction	h. semiconscious
9. f	between coasts	i. nonspecific
10. c	half a circle	j. international
11. i	not specific	k. semidry
12. g	between colleges	l. nonfactual

1. semicircle, intercollegiate, nonspecific
2. semicircle, nonspecific

page 78
1. triathlon
2. bifocals
3. multilingual
4. unicolor
5. bicentennial
6. unicorn
7. multicultural
8. trilogy
9. multipurpose

page 79
misunderstanding, mistreat, disobeying, misjudged, misled, discouraged, disappeared, displeased, misbehavior

page 80
Animation; positions; deception; calculations; attention; production; television
addition; illustrations; precision; concentration
invention; attraction

page 81
Answers will vary. Possible answers:
1. Mary Cassatt was a painter who often used women and children as her subjects.
2. The inventor's workshop was filled with all kinds of tools and parts.
3. The novelist will be signing books at the library on Friday.
4. The governor hopes to one day become president.
5. The biologist peered eagerly through the microscope, uncertain of what she might find.
6. Bryan has been a collector of White Sox memorabilia since he was seven.
7. Muhammad Ali was one of the greatest boxers of all time.
8. The conductor bowed to the audience, who gave her a standing ovation.

page 82
1. fairness; the state of being fair
2. occurrence; the act of occurring
3. assistance; the act of assisting
4. companionship; the state of being a companion
5. roundness; the state of being round
6. fragrance; the state of being fragrant
7. innocence; the state of being innocent
8. citizenship; the state of being a citizen

o	p	i	h	s	n	o	i	n	a	p	m	o	c
e	c	i	t	i	z	e	n	s	h	i	p	l	s
s	e	c	n	e	c	o	n	n	i	d	f	o	s
s	y	b	u	n	s	s	w	p	h	a	j	x	e
e	m	t	f	r	a	g	r	a	n	c	e	c	n
n	o	r	m	a	r	q	j	c	b	l	u	f	d
r	r	y	i	b	v	e	d	g	w	q	l	z	n
i	l	l	p	e	b	n	n	s	h	r	v	a	u
a	s	s	i	s	t	a	n	c	e	m	e	r	o
f	p	t	b	d	u	a	q	r	e	n	x	o	r

page 83
steamy; ancestral; finally; teary; grassy; brightly; traditional; magical; mossy; friendly; immediately; stuffy; musty; kindly; essential;

Answer Key

rainy; abruptly; inky; helpfully; cheery; thoughtfully; gently; approval

page 84

1. adventurous
   Aaron is very adventurous and loves to travel to exotic places.
2. infectious
   Courtney has an infectious laugh; anyone who hears it wants to laugh, too.
3. miraculous
   Tierra made a miraculous recovery from the flu, just in time for Nick's party.
4. cautious
   Zachary is cautious with money and always spends his allowance wisely.
5. ambitious
   If you are hardworking and ambitious, you will succeed in all that you do.
6. furious
   Hunter was furious when his new bike was stolen at the park.

1. ambitious, cautious, infectious
2. adventurous, miraculous, furious

page 85

1. Zoologic/al; education/al
2. expectant/ly; effortless/ly
3. graceful/ly; mossi/ness
4. fasten/er; cautious/ly
5. disgusting/ly; realist/ic
6. jerki/ly; strategic/al/ly
7. conversation/al; exceptional/ly
8. spotless/ness
9. companion/ship; playful/ly

page 86

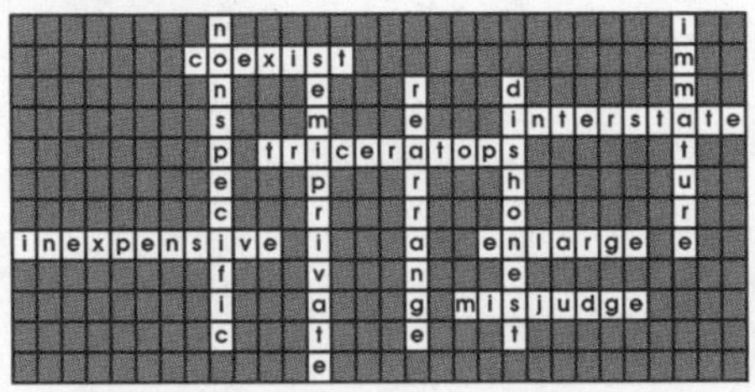

page 87

1. Depression
2. farmers, artists, teachers, hardships
3. competition
4. leadership
5. financial
6. explanation
7. slowly

page 88

1, 3, 2, 3, 2, 2, 1, 1, 2, 4, 3, 2, 1, 4, 3, 2, 3, 1, 3, 2, 2, 4, 3, 3, 3, 1, 1, 2

Find three bold words that contain the /ə/ sound. Write them on the lines and circle the letter or letters that make the sound. **Answers will vary. Possible answers:**

consider fungus dangerous

page 89

cup/cake; lem/on; ham/bur/ger; chim/ney a/corn; grass/hop/per; jel/ly/fish; plan/ets; i/ci/cles

page 90

sub/ma/rine, 3
pub/lic, 2; a/long, 2
mo/tor, 2; ve/hi/cle, 3
bal/loon, 2
steam/boat, 2; U/nit/ed, 3; Del/a/ware, 3
bi/cy/cles, 3; Scot/land, 2
lo/co/mo/tive, 4
street/car, 2
au/to/mo/bile, 4
air/plane, 2
hel/i/cop/ter, 4
su/per/son/ic, 4
com/ple/ted, 3
shut/tle, 2

page 91

2 **teaspoons** oil
½ pound chicken breast
7 ounces sliced **turkey** kielbasa
1 cup diced onion
1 diced green bell pepper
½ cup chopped **celery**
1½ cups **white** rice
3 cups chicken broth
2 teaspoons paprika
¼ teaspoon **ground** red pepper
½ teaspoon salt
1 teaspoon each dried **basil** and oregano
2 tablespoons tomato paste
1 can diced tomatoes with green chiles
½ pound cleaned, raw **shrimp**
¼ cup chopped green **onions**

1. Cut the chicken into little pieces. (Be sure to wash your hands **thoroughly** each time you touch raw meat or **seafood**.) Heat the oil in a large **saucepan**. Cook the chicken for about five minutes, and then transfer it to another dish.
2. Add the onion, pepper, and celery to the pan. Cook, **stirring** occasionally, for about 8 minutes. Add the kielbasa, and cook for an additional 5 minutes.
3. Add the rice, broth, and **seasonings** to the vegetable **mixture**. Bring it to a **boil**, then cover it and **reduce** the heat to low. Simmer for about 15 minutes.
4. Add the chicken, **tomato** paste, and diced tomatoes, and cook for 10 minutes.
5. Add the shrimp and green onions, and cook **just** until the shrimp turn pink.
6. **Garnish** with green onions, and serve with hot sauce. Recipe **yields** 6 servings.

Remember, you should always ask an **adult** for help in the kitchen when using knives or the stove.

page 92

1. recall
2. happen, quick
3. briefly
4. origin
5. probable

1. compliment, insult
2. question, answer
3. stiff, flexible
4. ancient, modern
5. public, private

page 93

cowardly, altered, viewpoint, motivated, group, finishing, previous, insignificant, failures, fortunately, vanished, always, located

page 94
1. failure
2. weak
3. slender
4. careless
5. empty
6. graceful
7. courageous
8. expand
9. stingy
10. often
11. wound
12. professional

1. A
2. S
3. A
4. A
5. S
6. S
7. A
8. A
9. S
10. A
11. S
12. A

page 95
1. opportunity
2. natural
3. amazing
4. completely
5. edges
6. permanent
7. reflected
8. harmful

page 96
1. Clear
   empty
2. tangled
   knotted
3. created
   invented
4. Divide
   Separate
5. power
   strength

page 97
changed; probably; lose; move; friends; stories; traveling; end; idea; a job; discovered; capture; home

page 98
1. mammal, dog, collie
2. place, city, Las Vegas
3. illness, disease, diabetes
4. subject, language, French
5. event, celebration, birthday
6. feeling, worry, panic
7. plant, tree, willow
8. vehicle, car, sedan
9. structure, building, stadium
10. currency, coin, dime

1. currency, language
2. language, French, birthday, feeling, building

page 99
1. ballet
2. sergeant
3. Orion
4. fork
5. teapots
6. novelist; pediatrician

1. duck
2. doghouse
3. flip-flop
4. bookcase
5. painting

page 100
Answers will vary. Possible answers: various, huge, transport, few, trustworthy, incredible, about, specific, depart, smart, exact, closer, certain, familiar, boring, artificial

page 101
1. demolish
   Answers will vary. Possible answer: Don't ruin the book for me by telling me what happens at the end.
2. dirty
   Answers will vary. Possible answer: The little girls spent all morning making mud pies in the backyard, and by lunchtime, their hands were filthy.
3. consume
   Answers will vary. Possible answer: I try to eat at least two pieces of fruit every day.
4. Remove
   Answers will vary. Possible answer: Delete the extra comma from the second paragraph of your report.
5. use
   Answers will vary. Possible answer: Do you know how to operate the new

DVD player?

6. turn

Answers will vary. Possible answer: The door revolves automatically, so be sure to keep moving.

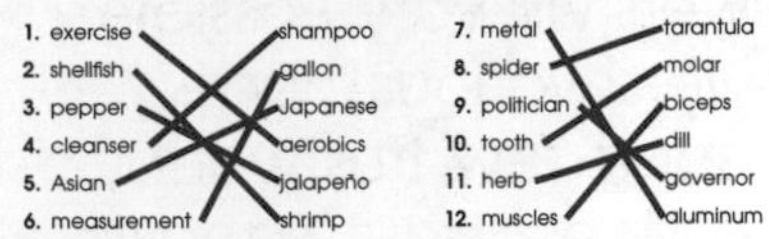

page 102

1. bolder, boulder
2. sore, soar
3. hoarse, horse
4. seller, cellar
5. wrung, rung
6. billed, build
7. flea, flee
8. aisle, isle
9. peddle, pedal

flea, flee

page 103

1. build
2. symbol
3. road
4. metal
5. sails
6. Capitol
7. side
8. seen

Answers will vary. Possible answers:

1. The chili simmered on the stove all afternoon.
   If you feel chilly tonight, there is an extra blanket in the closet.
2. The queen was sitting on her throne when the royal subjects entered the room.
   The slip of paper with Nicholas's phone number on it was accidentally thrown away.
3. The stationary bike has been sitting in our basement for at least two years.
   Anna makes her own customized stationery on the computer.

page 104

1. b
2. a
3. a
4. b
5. b
6. a

page 105

Answers will vary. Possible answers:

1. Strike the match against the side of the box.
2. The box of old records in the basement was damaged during the flood.
3. Kylie and Robert rode the Ferris wheel at the Bingham County Fair.
4. The cat's pupils were barely visible in the bright sunlight.
5. The baby in the photograph had a round, chubby face and pink cheeks.
6. The heroine of the book is my favorite character because she is kind to animals.
7. Although Michael's comment sounded mean, I don't think that is what he intended.
8. Can we go shopping for Bethany's birthday present after school today?

1. kind
2. round

page 106

bin; flee; there/they're; weather; fined; weigh; threw; cellars; close; flour; side; peace; bye/by; whole; knead; no

page 107

1. blocks
2. clubs
3. deck
4. story
5. objects
6. outlet

page 108

1. Zoological, Zoo
2. champion, champ
3. airplane, plane
4. mathematics, math
5. Gymnasium, Gym
6. professional, pro
7. hamburgers, burgers
8. limousine, limo
9. Miniature, Mini

1. champ, math
2. burgers

Answer Key

page 109
1. UFO
2. SCUBA
3. PTA
4. GPA
5. SUV
6. UNC
7. CIA

1. IMO
2. ASAP
3. LOL
4. BTW
5. OTOH
6. HAND

page 110
1. a
2. a
3. b
4. b
5. b
6. b
7. b
8. a

1. Paris
2. stack
3. more
4. moist
5. team
6. March
7. neon

page 111
1. brunch
2. Internet
3. dumbfound
4. splurged
5. smog
6. splattered
7. scrawl
8. guestimated; flurry

page 112
1. necktie
2. professor
3. examination
4. veterinarian
5. substitute
6. miniature
7. referee

1. BLT
2. IRS
3. POW
4. ASAP
5. VCR
6. MIT
7. RSVP
8. NATO

page 113
1. tell
2. save
3. drawn
4. race
5. frost

1. c
2. d
3. a
4. f
5. b
6. e

1. Medicare
2. fourteen
3. twirl
4. gleam

page 114
The sky was as perfectly blue as the inside of a swimming pool; absorbing the sights and sounds like sponges; His face...was as creased as a walnut; the octopus...inflate like a balloon; moving the strings like a puppeteer working a marionette; nearly a hundred kites filled the sky like bits of brightly-colored confetti; it soared effortlessly, like a hawk riding a current with outstretched wings

page 115
1. leaves; tiny hands
2. golf balls; round eggs
3. house; icebox
4. dog's tail; flag
5. seashells; tiny treasures
6. Davis; warrior
7. lights of the city; constellation

Possible answers: found, round, power, house, proudly

page 116
1. sunflowers dance
2. rays of the morning sun skip joyfully
3. mole looked anxiously at his watch
4. leaf sighed
5. night wind whistled, calling for a friend
6. cake beckoned invitingly
7. moped coughed, sputtered, gasping
8. camera eagerly captured each moment, tucking it away
9. The wind angrily rattled the windows.

10. chickadees, bickered.

1. Answers will vary.
2. Answers will vary.

page 117

As Juan and his father neared the lake, the paved road disappeared and two strips of gravel became their guide. <u>The crunch of the truck's tires across the rocks was like someone digging into a bag of potato chips.</u> Suddenly, Juan was hungry for lunch, even though it was only ten in the morning.

<u>The four-hour drive from home to the lake had flown by like school recess,</u> mostly because Juan was having so much fun. He and his dad jammed the radio, talked about sports, and <u>carried on like a couple of old fishing buddies.</u> This trip was only their second time out to the lake, but in some ways it felt like they'd been doing it forever.

Soon, the <u>boat drifted quietly through the fog like a leaf bobbing</u> along atop the waves. Juan's dad didn't say much. He was now a sea captain hunting for the best spot to drop anchor. Every few minutes, Juan asked if they could cast their lines yet. His dad told him that <u>he sounded like a broken record.</u>

Finally, Juan's dad steered the boat into a small area surrounded by foliage. All along the banks, tree branches hung down into the water. <u>They looked like divers</u> frozen at the moment they hit the surface.

Juan took a pole from his dad and smiled in anticipation. Then, <u>he cast his line into the water as if he had been asked to throw the first pitch at a baseball game</u>—the honor was more important than actually hitting the plate.

Before he knew it, though, Juan had a bite. The line became a laser beam cutting straight through the water's surface. Juan's dad told him to slowly reel the line in, a few turns at a time. <u>Like pulling a bucket from a well,</u> he lifted the fish out of the water and into the boat. Juan knew his lunch would be more than a bag of potato chips now.

page 118

Answers will vary. Possible answers:

1. Katrina got up on the wrong side of the bed this morning, but I'm sure that tomorrow will be a better day.
2. If I make the team, I promise to pull my own weight.
3. The uniforms cost an arm and a leg, but luckily, we've received quite a few donations.
4. Ellie is always willing to go the extra mile, so I know she'll work hard on this assignment.
5. Kathryn, give your mom a hand with the groceries.
6. Mr. Hoffmann is feeling under the weather so we will have a substitute teacher today.
7. I know it's been a hard week, but try to keep your chin up anyway.
8. Even though it was Samir's birthday, Leyla stole the spotlight when she performed her song for the guests.

page 119

1. made a beeline
2. piece of cake
3. fighting chance
4. just sail through
5. all thumbs
6. couldn't believe his eyes
7. down in the dumps
8. bent over backwards
9. In the blink of an eye

a fighting chance
down in the dumps
made a beeline
bent over backwards
all thumbs
a piece of cake
in the blink of an eye
couldn't believe his eyes
sail through

page 120

1. Increase
2. copy
3. foot
4. second
5. Often
6. March
7. student
8. carrots
9. food
10. cleaning
11. twenty-four
12. instrument
13. sweet

page 121

1. cow
2. baby
3. melt
4. Thermometer
5. United States
6. Sun

1. Green
2. spice
3. Centimeter
4. profit
5. needle
6. double
7. city
8. shell
9. airplane
10. chicken

page 122

1. Detroit
2. sport
3. lead
4. princess
5. web
6. seedling
7. bracelet
8. patients

1. e
2. a
3. f
4. e
5. d
6. c
7. b

page 123

1. *Sandpaper* feels rough, just as *silk* feels smooth.

2. *Thin* is a synonym for *slender*, just as *error* is a synonym for *mistake*.
3. A pedal is part of a bicycle, just as a hand is part of a clock.
4. Dishes are stored in a cupboard, just as a wrench is stored in a toolbox.
5. Nine is half of eighteen, just as thirteen is half of twenty-six.
6. *Stair* and *stare* are homophones, just as *towed* and *toad* are homophones.

Answers will vary. Possible answers:
1. *Present* is to *absent* as *shallow* is to *deep*.
2. *Nine* is to *ten* as *sixty-six* is to *sixty-seven*.
3. *Pea* is to *peanut* as *rain* is to *rainbow*.

page 124

1. S
2. M
3. S
4. M
5. M
6. S
7. S
8. S
9. M
10. S

Answers will vary. Possible answers:
1. From the airplane, the river looked like a necklace sparkling in the sunlight.
2. The sheet of blank paper that lay on the desk in front of Amelia was an invitation to write the best story she had ever written.
3. The darkness wrapped Rosie in a warm, comforting hug.

page 125

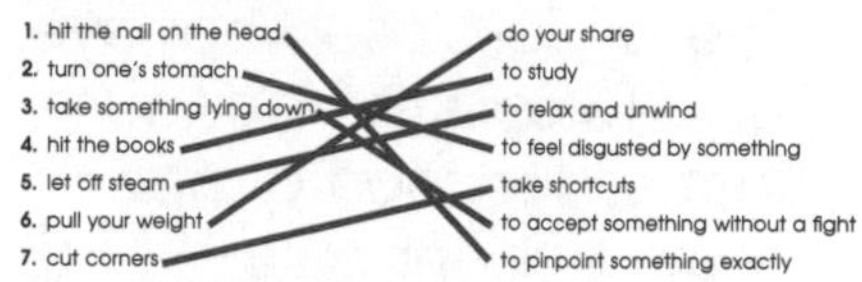

1. Aunt; uncle
2. Court; baseball
3. Wheel; rectangle
4. Matthew; Jenny
5. attraction; illustrate
6. circus; theater

page 126

1. a
2. b
3. a
4. b
5. b
6. b
7. a

page 127

1. cricket
2. contain
3. rub
4. dragonfly
5. divide
6. mosquito
7. find
8. soar

1. Answers will vary. Possible answer: Try not to squash the flowers when you are playing ball in the yard.
2. sincere
3. reflection * regal
4. five

page 128

1. a
2. b
3. b
4. c

<u>act</u>: actor, reacting, action
<u>create</u>: creation, recreation, creativity
<u>believe</u>: disbelief, unbelieving, believable
<u>admit</u>: admission, inadmissible, admitting

Possible answers: creation, recreation, action, admission

page 129

Answers will vary. Possible answers: begin; charity; misdirected; requested; helpful; shapeless; assistance; progression; worker; wasteful; reused; suggestion; feeling; disbelief

page 130

learn; attend; become; write; classroom; begin; notice; think; should; unique; light; spend; research; spell; appear; contain; entry

Answer Key

page 131

1. Answers will vary.
2. Answers will vary.
3. Answers will vary.
4. Answers will vary.
5. Answers will vary.

1. unexperienced, experience
2. realignible, align
3. irregularness, regular
4. ungreasiest, grease
5. misshippers, ship
6. reshapement, shape
7. misunderstatement, state
8. divisionalness, divide
9. semicouraged, courage
10. employingest, employ
11. naturing, nature
12. reneeding, need
13. reapproving, approve
14. prequotation, quote

page 132

1. cello
2. pumpernickel
3. cosmonaut
4. adios
5. origami
6. pajamas
7. bagel
8. ballet

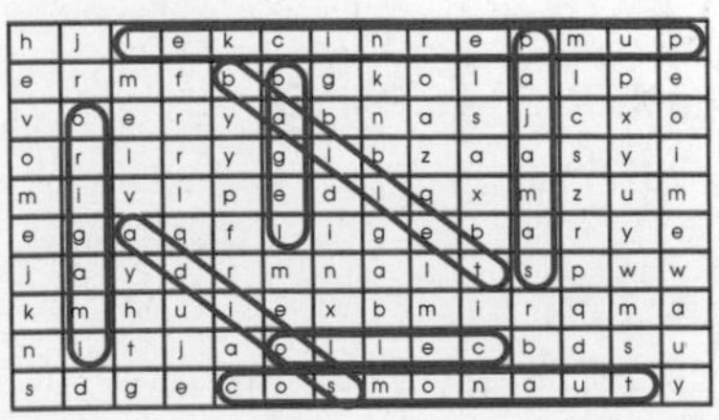

page 133

Sentences will vary. Possible answers:

1. German
The delicatessen at the corner of Fourth and Main makes excellent subs.
2. Spanish
Brad's aunt and uncle own a cattle ranch in Montana.
3. Yiddish
Can you make me a pastrami sandwich on rye bread?
4. French
The bride closed her eyes and tossed the bouquet in the direction of her maid of honor.
5. Japanese
Kris has been taking judo lessons for three years.
6. Italian
The carnival comes to town every August.
7. Australian (Aboriginal)
When it is thrown properly, the boomerang returns to the thrower.
8. Turkish
Baqir eats yogurt, granola, and a piece of fruit for breakfast every morning.

1. ranch, boomerang
2. judo, boomerang

page 134

1. umbrella
2. thunderstorm
3. Greek, Latin, French
4. create; Answers will vary. Possible answer: A poem is something that an author creates. It also is the product of being creative.
5. umbra

page 135

1. f
2. j
3. i
4. a
5. c
6. k
7. b
8. e
9. d
10. g
11. h

Answers may vary slightly, depending upon which dictionary a student uses.

1. from Middle English *educaten*, from Latin *ēducāre*
2. from French *oxygène*, from Greek *oxys*, *sharp*, or *acid*
3. from Middle English, from Old French, from Latin *serpēns*, from *serpere*, *to creep*
4. from Latin *plasticus*, from Greek *plastikos*, from *plassein*, *to mold*
5. from Middle English, from Old French *curios*, from Latin *cūriōsus*, from *cūra*, *to care*
6. from Italian, from Latin *zephirum*, from Arabic *ifr*, *nothing*
7. from Latin *continēns*, *continuous*, from

continēre, to hold together

8. after Gabriel Daniel Fahrenheit, German scientist

page 136

1. sherbet
2. kangaroo
3. magazine
4. jungle
5. potato
6. pickle
7. sled
8. typhoon
9. debris
10. carnival

page 137

1. to mutter
2. Greek, Latin, French, English
3. melidi; Answers will vary. Possible answer: When people sing, they usually follow a melody or a tune.

1. perfume
2. cookie
3. elevate
4. acrobat

elevate, acrobat, perfume

page 138

1. chronological
2. homophones
3. biography
4. tricycle
5. manual
6. thermos
7. Cyclops

1. recycling
2. chronicles
3. thermostat
4. symphony

page 139

1. meter
2. micro
3. ology
4. graph
5. ast
6. scope

1. the study of music
2. the study of the mind
3. the study of volcanoes
4. the study of animals
5. the study of myths

page 140

1. annual
2. auditorium
3. liberty
4. millipede
5. aquamarine
6. maritime
7. pedal

Answers will vary. Possible answer: year, liberty, bicycle

page 141

1. The Getty family subscribes to four magazines and two newspapers.
2. "My soccer team made it to the championship!" exclaimed Tyler.
3. It's hard for Leah to talk on the phone because her twin brothers are always interrupting.
4. Remember to subtract your expenses from your profits when you calculate the figures from the yard sale.
5. For his report on the history of transportation, Luis researched cars, trains, airplanes, and boats.

1. something, like a building, made up of assembled parts
   Although the structure was nearly two hundred years old, it was still strong and sturdy.
2. to burst, release, or explode
   The students watched the volcano erupt on the television screen.
3. to write an order for medicine
   Did the doctor prescribe anything for your infection?
4. able to be carried from one place to another
   Lexi saved all the money she made babysitting and bought a portable MP3 player on sale.

page 142

1. G, thermos
2. L, construct
3. L, porter
4. G, biography
5. L, audition
6. G, chronological
7. G, homophones

page 143

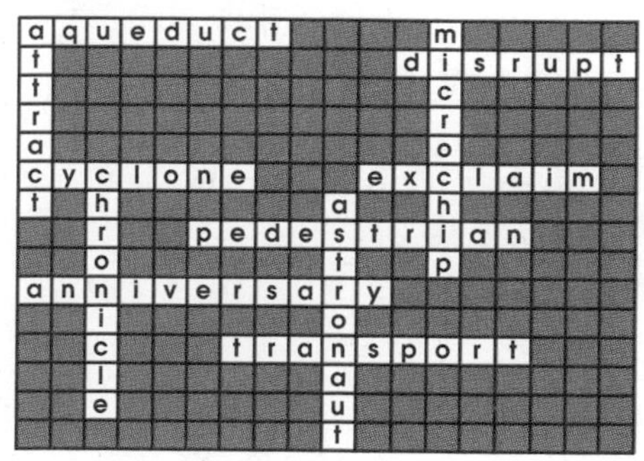

page 144

1. b
2. a
3. a
4. c

5. b
6. c
7. a

page 145

different, styles, heard, combines, melodies, folk, traditional, rhythmic, accompanies, guitar, classical, usually, instrument, upbeat, religious, brought, region, percussion, years, quietly

page 146

cider; juice; cinnamon; ginger; processor; cookie; pieces; softened; evaporates; fruit; leather; applesauce; oven; ready; stored; increase

page 147

1. in trist; tal ənt
2. trān ing; prə fesh ə nəlz
3. rā shəl lē; di rek tər
4. māk; thrü; kul cher
5. kum pə nē; ə mâr i kən
6. kə mū ni kāt; rās
7. ə mung; wûrld

professionals, racially

page 148

1. a
2. a
3. b
4. a
5. b

1. One of the best things you can do to help the /**en vī′ren ment**/ is to reduce, reuse, and /**rē sī′kel**/.
2. Make your /**pā′per**/ last twice as long by printing on the back of each page.
3. /**in sted′**/ of buying /**bôt′ld**/ water in plastic bottles, bring your own /**rē ūz′e bel**/ water jug with you /**hwâr ev′er**/ you go.
4. /**dō′nāt**/ clothes you've outgrown to /**châr′i tēz**/, or cut them into rags that can be used in place of paper /**tou′elz**/.
5. Read /**lā′belz**/, and use products made from recycled /**me tēr′ē elz**/.
6. If you /**viz′it**/ someplace that doesn't recycle, write a letter telling the /**kum′pe nē**/ it's important to you and /**ik splān′ing**/ how they can get started.

page 149

1. /ə kôm′ ə dā′shenz/
2. /hel′ə kôp′ tər/
3. /ra′snāk′/
4. /lō′ kə mō′shen/
5. /wō′hut′/
6. /sun′bôd′ ē/
7. /gâr′ ən tē′/
8. /pâr tis′ə pāt′/

1. b a
2. a b
3. a b
4. b a
5. b a
6. a b
7. b a

page 150

kas′ əl
el′ ə fənt
kə nü′
kəm pū′ tər
gi tär′
brôk′ ə lē
tor nā′ dō
bə nan′ ə
ham′ ək

1. Local Teen Wins (rē je′ nel, rē′ je nel) Spelling Championship
2. (hev ē′, hev′ ē) Weekend Storms Knock Out Power to 150,000 Residents
3. Clausen Withdraws from Race Three Weeks Before (i lek′ shen, i lek shen′)
4. Plans for New East Side Shopping Mall—Why Are (pē pel′, pē′ pel) Protesting?
5. (mi stêr′ ē es, mi′ stêr ē es) Briefcase Found Containing $2,000
6. (lō′ kel, lō kel′) Funding Cuts Mean Arts School May Have to Shut Its Doors
7. (e non′ e mes, e non e mes′) Donor Contributes $45,000 to Renovation of Kaufmann Theater
8. Hollywood Comes to Town for Filming of New (ak shen′, ak′ shen) Flick

page 151

1. Chislehurst Caves, located in a suburb of London, are /**ak chü e lē**/ actually former chalk and flint mines.
2. No one is sure exactly how old the caves are, but the /**ûr lē ist**/ earliest known /**ref er ens**/ reference to them is A.D. 1250.
3. The caves /**in klüd**/ include approximately 22 miles of /**tun elz**/ tunnels and passageways.
4. The depth of the caves /**vār ēz**/ varies from 40 feet below the /**sûr fes**/ surface to about 150 feet underground.
5. The temperature of the caves remains /**sted ē**/ steady, summer or winter, at 45 /**di grēz**/ degrees Fahrenheit.
6. The last time the caves were used as mines was in the 1830s, but they have had many /**uth er**/ other uses since that time.
7. Mushrooms grow well in dark, damp /**plā sez**/ places, so for some time the caves were used as a sort of mushroom farm.
8. During World War II, the caves were turned into an /**e māz ing**/ amazing underground /**sit ē**/ city.
9. They were a /**ken vēn yent**/ convenient air raid shelter for Londoners.
10. The caves were wired for /**i lek tris i tē**/ electricity and contained a /**hôs pi tl**/ hospital, chapel, movie theater and gym.
11. During the war, the caves were filled with about 15,000 people seeking shelter /**ev rē**/ every night.